Translators   : Yoko Yagasaki
                Yoko Ishiguro
English Editor : Mieko Baba

Fabric Materials per Branch:
Flowers/Buds : 30" x 6" pink crepe fabric
Branch : 2" x 1.2 yds brown cotton

1　CHERRY BLOSSOMS
【Rose Family】
Floral language: Spiritual beauty
Cherry blossoms made with crepe fabric. Rustic effect is enhanced by using hand-torn brown fabric to cover the branch. A piece that you may like to arrange prior to the arrival of spring.

Preparation: Referring to page 78, cut necessary numbers of fabric parts.

To assemble, you will need: 3 #20 stem wires, 7 #28 stem wires, Facial tissue, 50 stamens, Green floral tape, Silk button thread (ash green), Awl, Craft glue

Make Blossoms

1. Place 2 pieces of petal fabric together, right sides facing in, and work a running stitch 1/8" inside. Make a cut in the center of the back of petal, and turn petal right side out. On the right side, work stem stitches of ash green thread in a star shape.

2. Stitch a circle in the center of the star. Leave the thread attached. Using an awl, make a hole in the center of the circle.

3. Fold 10 stamens in half, and hook them with a #28 wire bent in half. Twist wire tightly to secure, and insert through the hole made in the petal.

4. Pull the hanging thread left with the petal tightly to gather. Wind firmly the thread around the base of petal, and knot off to secure. Make 5.

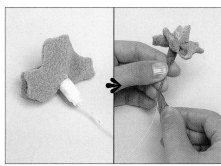

5. Wrap tissue around the base of flower, and cover it with floral tape.

Make Buds

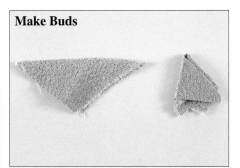

6. Fold bud fabric in half to make a triangle. Fold down both peaks, so the middle of the original fold makes the apex.

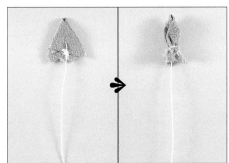

7. Cut 4" length of #28 wire and attach it to the lower part of the bud with glue. Wrap wire with the fabric and wind thread tightly around it to secure. Make 6.

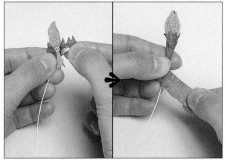

8. Cut a zigzag pattern on one side of floral tape. Apply glue onto tape and attach to the base of bud. Tape down.

Make Branch

9. Assemble 3 stems of flowers. Tear the branch fabric into long strips. Place some glue on one and wrap around the 3 stems. Follow the same procedure to assemble 4 buds together.

10. Join three #20 wires, and start wrapping it with tissue paper at 1/3 from the top, gradually adding thickness toward the bottom. Using the stem fabric, attach the remaining flowers and buds on top of the wire, then randomly attach the 3-flower stem and 4-bud stem made in Step 9.

Completion

11. When you reach the bottom end, cover the bottom with fabric, and wrap upward a few times and glue to secure.

●For easy comprehension, threads are shown in contrasting colors. When making actual projects, select matching shades for each fabric.

2 TULIP

【Lily Family】

Floral language: Caring

Tulips made in coordinated pale pink fabrics. Half-hidden flower centers made of beads add an elegant atmosphere.

Fabric Materials per Stem:
Petals : 20" x 4" solid color fabric (A)
20" x 4" printed fabric (B)
Leaf/Stem : 14" x 8" solid color fabric

Preparation: Referring to page 78, cut necessary numbers of fabric and other parts.

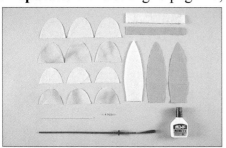

To assemble, you will need: 4" x 8" quilt batting, 1" x 8" batting strip, 1 #18 stem wire, 5 4mm beads, #2 (3/16") tube turner, Craft glue

Make Stem

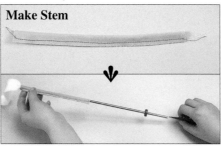

1. Fold stem fabric lengthwise in half, right sides facing in and stitch along the long side, 3/8" from the fold. Insert a tube turner into the fabric tube and push in the batting strip as you turn the fabric right side out. Stitch to secure cording to one end of this tube.

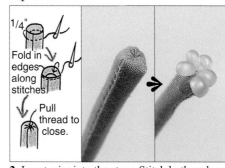

2. Insert wire into the stem. Stitch both ends as shown. Sew on 5 beads on one end of stem.

Make Flower

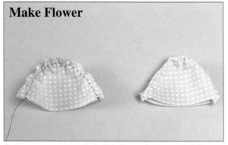

3. Layer one petal A fabric and one petal B fabric right sides facing in and gather-stitch at 1/4" inside of raw edges. Pull thread lightly to gather fabric and knot off to secure. Turn right side out. Make 3 large petals and 3 small ones.

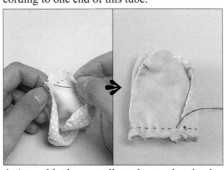

4. Assemble three small petals, overlapping by half, and gather-stitch at 1/4" inside of lower edge to make a thick tube. Leave thread attached. Repeat with large petals.

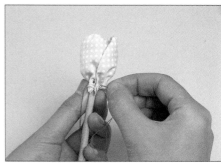

5. Turn petal tube so that printed side faces out. Insert stem wire with beads through the petals and pull thread tightly to gather petals around the stem. Stitch to the stem.

6. Insert large petals, upside down, through the stem wire. Pull thread tightly to gather petals around the stem. Stitch to the stem.

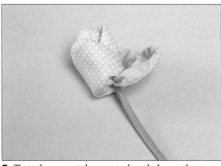

7. Turn large petals upward and shape the form. Glue inside of large petals onto small petals.

Make Leaf

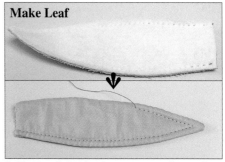

8. Place quilt batting between two pieces of leaf fabric, right sides facing in. Stitch at 1/8" inside of raw edges, leaving opening unstitched. Turn right side out. Stitch around leaf, 1/4" inside.

Attach Leaf

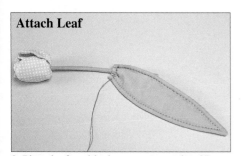

9. Place leaf upside down on stem wire, 2" from wire end. Attach leaf to stem by stitching across tightly 1/4" inside of raw edges. Pull thread to gather leaf and knot off to secure.

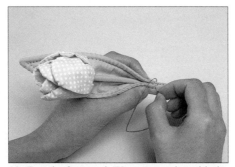

10. Turn leaf upward. Wrap stem wire with the leaf, so the lower sides butt each other, and slipstitch about 1" from the bottom of leaf to secure.

Completion

11. Make different combinations of patterns and solids for the petals, carefully choosing similar tones.

●For easy comprehension, threads are shown in contrasting colors. When making actual projects, select matching shades for each fabric.

Fabric Materials per Stem:
Petals : 16" x 8" cotton
Leaf/Stem : 16" x 16" cotton

3 TULIP
【Lily Family】
Floral language: Declaration of love
**Cheerful tulips bloom in many colors.
Let each flower bloom softly by using
your favorite scrap fabric.**

Preparation: Referring to page 79, cut necessary numbers of fabric and other parts.

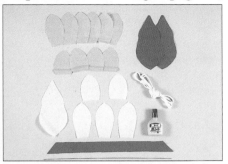

To assemble, you will need: 16" x 20" adhesive interlining, 2 #16 bare stem wires, 14" round cording (³/₈" diam.), Craft glue

Make Stem

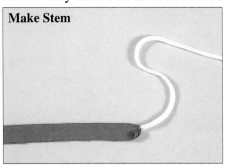

1. Fold stem fabric lengthwise in half, right sides facing in. Stitch along the length, ¹/₄" from raw edges. Stitch to secure cording to one end of this tube.

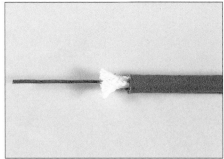

2. Using a tube turner, turn the fabric inside out, while filling the stem with cording. Insert two wires into the stem.

Make Flower

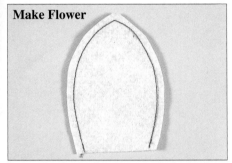

3. Attach adhesive interlining to the back of one petal A fabric. Layer another petal A fabric, right sides facing in, and stitch through all three layers, ¹/₄" inside the raw edge. Leave opening unstitched. Layer and stitch petal B alike.

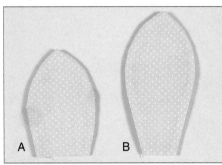

4. Turn petal right side out. Make 2 petal A and 3 petal B.

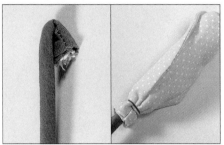

5. Bend ³/₈" end of stem. Make tucks on lower part of the 2 petals A and attach them 2" below the bend of wire. Wind thread tightly around the base of petals to secure. Apply some glue where petals overlap.

6. Make tucks on the lower part of the three petals B. Attach them to stem wire below petals A but upside down. Wind thread tightly around the base of petals to secure.

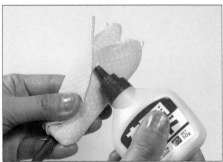

7. Fold petals B upward to cover petals A. Apply some glue where petals overlap.

Make Leaf

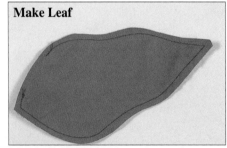

8. In the same manner as petals, attach adhesive interlining to the back of one leaf fabric. Stitch together right sides facing in, ¹/₄" from raw edge. Leave opening unstitched.

9. Make slits where seams curve. Turn leaf right side out. Slipstitch to close opening.

Attach Leaf

10. Attach leaf at 6" from base of flower. Wrap the stem with leaf at about 6" below the base of flower, and glue to secure.

Completion

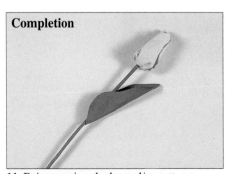

11. Enjoy varying shades and/or patterns.

● For easy comprehension, threads are shown in contrasting colors. When making actual projects, select matching shades for each fabric.

Fabric Materials per Stem:
Petals : 8" x 2" solid color cotton (A)
6" x 2" checked pattern cotton (B)
Small center : 2" x 2" yellow cotton
Large center : 2" x 2" purple cotton
Leaf/Stem/Calyx: 4" x 8" cotton

4 PANSY
【Viola Family】
Floral language: Reverie, Think of me
Very charming flower with heads slightly
drooping when in bloom. Also called
"viola tricolor". Mix and match colors
and patterns for appealing presentation.

Preparation: Referring to page 79, cut necessary numbers of fabric parts.

To assemble, you will need: 1/2" x 14" batting strip, 1 #20 green stem wire, Craft glue

Make Center of Flower

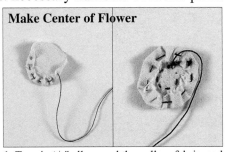

1. Turn in 1/4" all around the yellow fabric, and stitch along edges, gathering roughly. Stitch in the round again, 1/8" inside of previously folded edge. Pull thread to gather. Prepare large purple center in the same manner.

2. Cut stem wire into 6" and bend one end into a loop. With an awl, make a hole in the middle of both small and large centers. Insert wire through the centers.

3. Starting from the underside of centers, wrap wire with batting strip thickly layering over the previous wrap. Glue ends to secure.

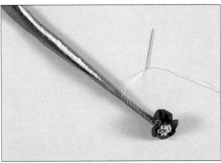

4. Wrap stem fabric around wrapped wire and slipstitch to secure. Fold in both ends of fabric.

Make Flower

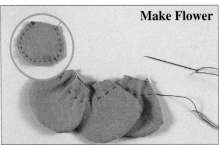

5. Layer 2 pieces of petal fabric right sides facing in, and stitch 1/8" inside. Leave opening unstitched. Turn right side out. Make 3 petals with fabric A and 2 with fabric B. Join petals of fabric A as shown. Repeat with fabric B. Leave thread attached.

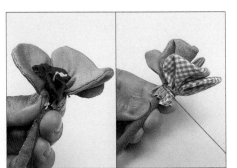

6. Attach fabric A petals to the base of center and stitch to secure. Attach fabric B petals over A and stitch to secure. Pull thread tightly.

Make Calyx

7. Turn in 1/4" of calyx fabric and stitch along the edges, gathering as you go. Pull thread lightly to give it some body.

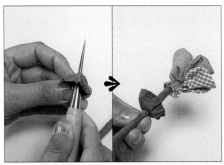

8. With an awl, make a hole in the middle of the calyx. Insert completed stem through the hole.

9. Slipstitch to secure calyx to the back of petals.

Make Leaf

10. Work running stitch around 2 pieces of leaf fabric, right sides facing in, 1/8" from raw edges. Leave opening unstitched. Turn right side out. Slipstitch to close the opening. Attach leaf 2" below the base of calyx and slipstitch to secure.

Completion

11. Assort matching colors and patterns of petals.

●For easy comprehension, threads are shown in contrasting colors. When making actual projects, select matching shades for each fabric.

5 GARDEN STOCK

【Mustard Family】
Floral language: Eternal beauty

A refreshing flower with long stem. Pale pastel colored flannel conveys a homely impression.

Fabric Materials per Stem
Petals/Buds : 14" x 18" flannel
Leaves : 6" x 8" cotton

Preparation: Referring to page 80, cut necessary numbers of fabric parts.

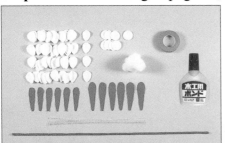

To assemble, you will need: 8 #22 white stem wires, 1 extra-thick stem wire(1/4") cut to 20" length, Polyfil, Green floral tape, Craft glue, Chemical laundry starch

Make Florets

1. Cut #22 stem wire into 2 1/4" -length. Attach 4 pieces of flower fabric to stem wire and wrap with floral tape. Prepare 25 florets.

Make Buds

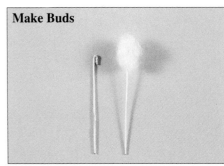

2. Cut stem wire into 2 1/4" -length. Bend 1/4" of one end of wire into a loop. Wrap polyfil around wire and glue to secure.

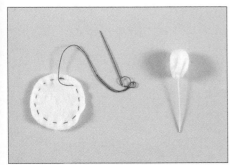

3. Work running-stitch around bud fabric, 1/4" from raw edges. Cover bud stem wire with bud fabric and pull thread to gather. Stitch to secure.

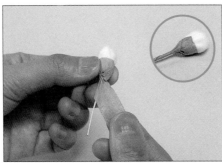

4. Wrap bud stem with floral tape to cover stitches. Make 8 buds.

Attach Buds

5. Attach buds to extra-thick stem wire with floral tape. Make 2 rows of 4 buds each, 3/4" apart.

Attach Florets

6. Attach 5 rows of 4 florets with floral tape, 3/4" apart, then end with a row of 5 florets for the bottom row.

7. Make a 10% solution of chemical laundry starch. Dip flower into the solution and squeeze excess.

8. Carefully unfold blossoms while still damp, and shape the form.

Make Leaves

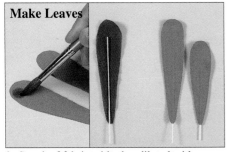

9. Coat leaf fabric with glue diluted with double amount of water. Cut #22 wire into 4" length for large leaf and 3" length for small leaf. Place wire in the middle of two pieces of leaf fabric and glue together.

Attach Leaves

10. Starting at 1" from the underside of the last row of blossoms, attach 2 rows of 3 leaves in varied sizes with floral tape.

Completion

11. Adapt by changing shades of petals.

●For easy comprehension, threads are shown in contrasting colors. When making actual projects, select matching shades for each fabric.

13

Fabric Materials per Stem:
Petals : 14" x 4" printed fabric (A)
: 14" x 4" solid color fabric (B)
Stem : 8" x 8" solid color fabric

6 SWEET PEA
【Pea Family】
Floral language: Godspeed
**Soft rippling petals are part of
its attractiveness. Select pastel
hues to add elegance and grace.**

Preparation: Referring to page 80, cut necessary numbers of fabric parts.

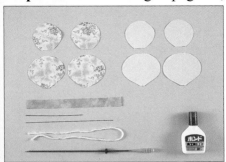

To assemble, you will need: 18" bulky wool yarn, 1 #20 stem wire, #1 (1/8") tube turner, Craft glue

Make Flowers

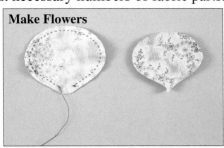

1. Layer one piece each of petal fabric A and B, right sides facing in, and stitch 1/4" inside of raw edges. Leave 1/2" at the bottom unstitched to use as opening. Turn right side out. Repeat to make 2 large and 2 small petals.

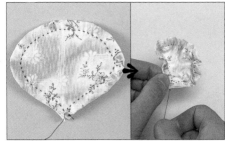

2. Stitch tightly around the edge of large petal, 1/4" inside the edge. Place printed side of petal up and pull thread lightly to make gathers. Knot off to secure. Repeat with small petals.

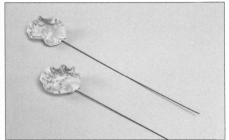

3. Cut one 8" piece, and one 5" piece of #20 stem wire. Place a 3/8" line of glue on top of wires. Insert both wires through the openings of the two small petals.

4. Place some glue at the base of small petals and pinch the sides of the petals with your fingers to secure.

5. Stitch 1/4" above the opening of large petal, edge to edge. Leave thread attached. Fold in and place some glue on the 1/4" seam at opening.

6. Place small petal inside large petal. Pull thread tightly to gather both petals. Pinch the edges of large petal together and slipstitch to secure, 3/8" from bottom of petal.

Make Stem

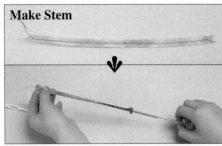

7. Fold stem fabric lengthwise in half, and stitch along the center. Fold the 18" wool yarn in half. Insert a tube turner into the fabric tube and push in the wool yarn as you turn the fabric right side out.

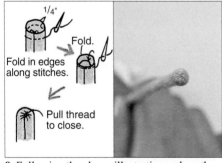

1/4"

Fold in edges along stitches.

Fold.

Pull thread to close.

8. Following the above illustrations, close the bottom part of stem fabric.

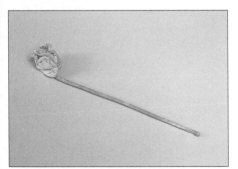

9. Insert the 8" stem wire with petals into the stem tube. Stitch to close the top of stem referring to illustrations in Step 8.

10. Make a hole on the stem with an awl, 3" below the petals. Insert the 5" wire with petals into it.

Completion

11. Bend the wired stem to add movement to the flower.

●For easy comprehension, threads are shown in contrasting colors. When making actual projects, select matching shades for each fabric.

Fabric Materials per Stem:
Petals/Center of flower B : 14" x 6" pink fabric
Center of flower A : 2" x 2" yellow fabric
Stem/Calyx : 8" x 6" solid color fabric

7 GERBERA
【Chrysanthemum Family】
Floral language: Mysteriousness
**Garberas will multiple pastel petals
and large centers will provide warmth
and cheerfulness to your room.**

*Arrange with tulips for a change.
Blended warm tones give a
sophisticated air.*

16

Preparation: Referring to page 81, cut necessary numbers of fabric and other parts.

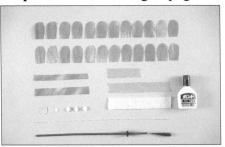

To assemble, you will need: 1" x 8" batting strip, 1/2" x 2" quilt batting, 2" x 3/8" cardboard, 1 #18 stem wire, #2 (3/16") tube turner, Craft glue

Make Petals

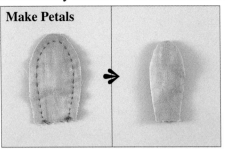

1. Layer 2 pieces of petal fabric, right sides facing in, and stitch 1/8" inside of raw edges. Leave opening unstitched. Turn right side out, and adjust the shape of petal. Make 12 petals.

2. Overlap petals by half and arrange 12 petals into a circle. Stitch 1/4" inside of inner edges to assemble petals together. Pull thread tightly.

Make Center of Flower A

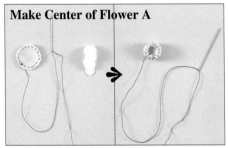

3. Work a tight running stitch along the edges of flower-center fabric, 1/8" inside. Layer 3 pieces of quilt batting and cardboard in the center of fabric. Pull thread tightly.

Make Center of Flower B

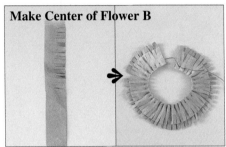

4. Cut 3/8"- deep slashes 1/8" apart into outer stamen fabric. Cut 1/4"- deep slashes 1/8" apart for inner stamen fabric. Layer both pieces of fabric and stitch together 1/4" inside of the opposite edge to form a circle.

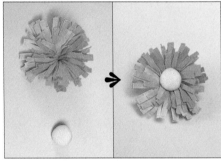

5. Pull thread tightly and knot off. Attach center of flower A with glue.

Completed form of Flower

6. Attach center of flower to petals with glue.

Make Stem

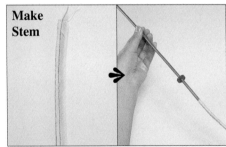

7. Fold stem fabric lengthwise in half and stitch along the edge, 3/16" from the fold. Insert a tube turner into the fabric tube and push in batting strip as you turn fabric right side out. Refer to page 76 for the use of tube turner.

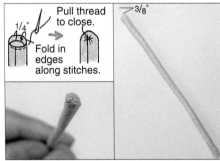

8. Finish bottom of stem as shown. Insert stem wire into the stem tube. Trim wire at 3/8" longer than the length of stem tube.

Make Calyx

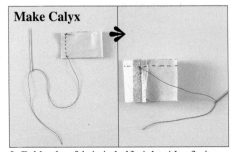

9. Fold calyx fabric in half, right sides facing in, and work running-stitch along the side, 1/4" from raw edges, to make a tube. Open the seam and work a running-stitch along the top edge, 1/4" inside.

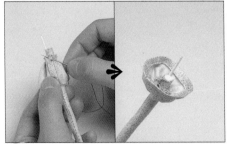

10. Insert stem through calyx fabric, stitched side up. The stitched line should be 1/4" below the edge of stem fabric. Pull thread of calyx to gather fabric and stitch to secure . Turn calyx upward. Turn in 1/4" around the top of calyx fabric.

Attach Flower

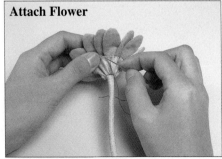

11. Apply some glue onto tip of wire and attach to blossom. Slipstitch to secure calyx to underside of petals to finish.

●For easy comprehension, threads are shown in contrasting colors. When making actual projects, select matching shades for each fabric.

Fabric Materials per Stem:
Petals : 10" x 10" cotton
Leaf/Calyx : 6" x 4" cotton

8 CARNATION
【Dianthus Family】
Floral language: Mother's love
**A flower which can't be
missed on Mother's Day.
A hand-made single stem will
make a wonderful gift.**

Preparation: Referring to page 82, cut necessary numbers of fabric parts. To add stiffness to fabric, coat each part with glue diluted with double amount of water, then let dry completely.

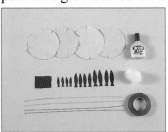

To assemble, you will need: 2 #20 green stem wire, 1 #26 green stem wire, Polyfil, Craft glue, Green floral tape

Make Flower

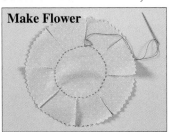

1. Work running-stitches in the round on petal fabric, just inside the slit ends. Leave thread attached.

2. Pull thread to gather fabric. Wind the remaining thread around the base of petal. Knot off. Make 4.

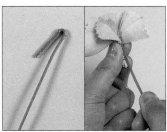

3. Bend 3/8" end of stem wire into a hook. Hook wire securely through the slits of one floret.

4. Add the remaining 3 florets one by one, by stitching tightly to secure.

5. Wind thread tightly around the base of the 4 florets.

6. Wrap a thin layer of polyfil around the base of the flower.

Make Calyx

7. Fold calyx fabric in half, right sides facing in, and stitch along the raw edge, 1/8" inside.

8. Gather stitch along the bottom edge of calyx fabric tube, 1/8" inside. Leave thread attached.

9. Insert wire through the calyx fabric, bottom-side up. Pull thread tightly around wire.

10. Turn calyx fabric upward and neatly cover the polyfil at the base of the flower. Use an awl to facilitate work.

11. Secure calyx by gluing its upper edges to the base of flower.

Make Leaves

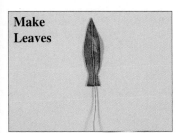

12. Coat back side of leaf fabric with glue, place a 2 1/4" stem wire in the middle of the leaf and cover it with another piece of leaf fabric.

13. Make 2 each of large, medium, and small-size leaves.

Attach Leaves

14. Attach with floral tape 2 small leaves right below the calyx. Attach medium and large leaves at 2 1/2" intervals.

Completion

15. Showing the completed carnation.

●For easy comprehension, threads are shown in contrasting colors. When making actual projects, select matching shades for each fabric.

Fabric Materials per Stem:
Petals : 14" x 10" cotton
Stem/Calyx/Leaves : 24" x 6" cotton

9 ROSE
【Rose Family】
Floral language: True love, Passion
Large roses bloom gracefully in their full glory. Add variation to texture by using different materials like light cotton or cotton velvet.

Preparation: Referring to page 82, cut necessary numbers of fabric parts. To add stiffness to fabric, coat each part with glue diluted with double amount of water, then let dry completely.

To assemble, you will need:
2" x 4" stocking scrap, 8 #26 green stem wires, Polyfil, Craft glue

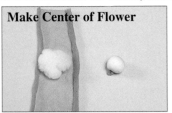

Make Center of Flower

1. Wrap polyfil with a 2" x 4" piece of stocking to make a 1" ball. Tie ends of stocking and trim off excess.

2. Insert a 14" stem wire through the ball below the knot. Insert another 14" stem wire across the first. Bend down the wires to wrap the ball and twist all four wires. This makes the center of flower.

Make Flower

3. Moisten petal fabric with water. Crumple to form creases then spread on a surface.

4. Using a toothpick, curl all edges of 4 petals inward. Leave one piece of small petal fabric uncurled.

5. Using an awl, make a hole in the center of the uncurled petal fabric. Insert the wire of flower center through the hole. Wrap petals around the center of flower and glue to secure.

6. Make a hole in the center of the other small petal fabric and insert center of flower through it. Glue petals to the first one. Make sure that petals do not overlap.

7. Make a hole in the center of the remaining 3 large petal pieces. Attach them to the small petals. All petals should be staggered and opened when glued on.

8. Twist the tips of calyx fabric with your fingers.

9. Make a hole in the center of calyx with an awl. Insert flower stem through the hole. Apply some glue on calyx and attach it to underside of flower.

10. Wrap the stem with stem fabric starting at 1" below the calyx. Wrap upward at a slight angle, and wrap a few more times to thicken top part and glue end to secure.

Make Leaves

11. Moisten leaf fabric with water. Crumple to form creases then flatten on a surface. Attach stem wire to the back of each leaf with glue. Make 2 large leaves and 4 small leaves.

12. Wrap and glue stem fabric around the wire of large leaf.

13. Attach two small leaves 1" below the large leaf. Continue wrapping and gluing stem fabric for a further 2".

Attach Leaves

14. Start wrapping stem fabric from the underside of calyx. Attach two leaf units at 2" intervals and continue wrapping to the end of the wire.

Completion

15. To make a gift decoration shown on the opposite page, shorten the stem and add only one leaf unit.

●For easy comprehension, threads are shown in contrasting colors. When making actual projects, select matching shades for each fabric.

Fabric Materials per Stem:
Petals/Bud : 40" x 12" silky fabric
Leaves/Stem/Calyxes : 12" x 10" solid color fabric

10 ROSE
【Rose Family】
Floral language: Modesty
Soft and fluffy rose blossoms created with peach color fabric. Hand-stitched leaves further enhance the warm atmosphere.

Preparation: Referring to page 83, cut necessary numbers of fabric and other parts.

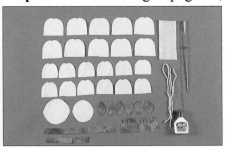

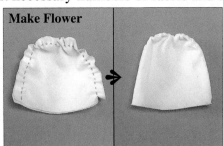
Make Flower

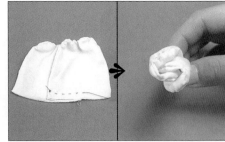

To assemble, you will need: 4" x 4" quilt batting, 1.2 yds wool yarn (extra thick), 2 #20 stem wires, #1 (1/8") tube turner, Craft glue

1. Layer 2 pieces of petal fabric, right sides facing, and stitch 1/4" inside. Pull thread lightly to gather around the top of fabric and turn fabric right side out. Make 5 large petals and 6 small ones.

2. Layer 2 small petals, overlapping by half, and stitch together to form a tube, 1/4" inside of bottom edge. Pull thread tightly. Knot off.

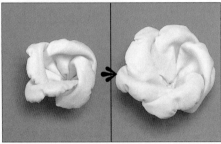

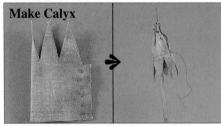
Make Calyx

3. In the same manner as Step 2, join 4 small petals into a cup. Join 5 large petals alike. Leave threads attached.

4. Place the 2 small-petal unit into the 4 small-petal cup. Pull thread tightly and stitch to secure. Place this unit into the 5 large-petal cup and pull thread tightly. Stitch to secure for completed blossom.

5. Fold calyx fabric in half, right sides facing in, and stitch along side edge, 1/4" inside. Stitch sideways at 1/4" along the straight edge. Leave threads attached. Make stem referring to page 15. Insert wire into the stem. Cut wire 1/2" longer than stem. Insert stem through calyx fabric held upside down. At 1/4" under the base of flower, pull the upper thread tightly, and stitch to secure.

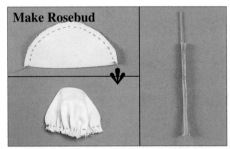
Make Rosebud

6. Apply glue on the tip of wire and insert it into the base of the flower. Turn calyx upward and glue onto the fabric by gluing at several points. Pull the remaining thread slightly to gather fabric, and stitch to secure.

7. Fold rosebud fabric in half and stitch around the edges, 1/4" inside. Pull thread to gather to about 2"- width. Prepare inner and outer petals of bud. Make rosebud stem referring to page 15 and insert a 10"-long wire. Cut wire 1" longer than the stem tube.

8. Form calyx in the same manner as blossom, and attach to the stem wire. Apply glue along the bottom edge of small rosebud fabric and wrap it around the glued part of the wire.

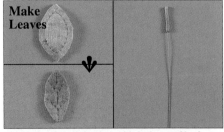
Make Leaves

Attach Leaves

9. Wrap outer rosebud fabric around the inner one. Turn calyx upward and glue to secure. Pull the remaining thread lightly to gather fabric, and stitch to secure.

10. Sandwich quilt batting with 2 pieces of leaf fabric right sides facing in. Stitch through all three layers, 1/4" inside, leaving opening unstitched. Turn right side out and slipstitch to close opening. Embroider the veins. Make stem referring to page 15. Stitch to close the top side of leaf stem. Insert a 5" length of wire.

11. Slipstitch leaves to stem as shown above. Using an awl, make a hole on the flower stem, and insert stems of rosebud and leaves. Slipstitch around the joint for finished flower.

●For easy comprehension, threads are shown in contrasting colors. When making actual projects, select matching shades for each fabric.

11 BABY'S BREATH

【Dianthus Family】

Floral language: Pure heart

Countless small florets bloom like a haze and are very romantic. Beautiful on its own but more attractive when combined with other flowers.

A bouquet of roses and baby's breath: You can create beautiful bouquets by combining two or more kinds of flowers, like here, roses and baby's breath.

Fabric Materials per Stem:

Petals: 4" x 2" cotton lace

Preparation: Referring to page 84, cut necessary numbers of fabric parts.

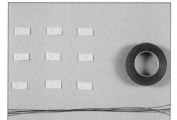

To assemble, you will need: 3 #28 green stem wires, Green floral tape

★Cut stem wires into three sizes: A= 14" (1 piece), B=7" (2 pieces), C= 5" (3 pieces)

1. Bend 3/8" end of wires A and B. Bend 3/8" of both ends of wire C. Catch one petal fabric in the wire hook. Twist wire tightly to secure. Attach petal fabric on both ends of wire C.

2. Bring up both sides of petal fabric, and wrap the base of flowers with floral tape to cover the twisted wire.

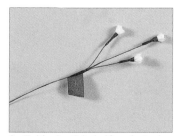

3. Fold wire C in half, and attach to wire B. Wrap about 1" around the joint with floral tape. Make two of this unit.

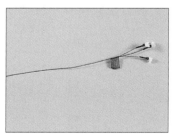

4. Fold wire C in half and attach to wire A. Wrap 1" around the joint with floral tape.

5. Assemble 2 stems made in Step 3 and 1 stem made in Step 4. Wrap about 1" around the joint with floral tape. Trim edges of florets with pinking shears.

Completion

6. Arrange the shape of stems as desired.

●For easy comprehension, threads are shown in contrasting colors. When making actual projects, select matching shades for each fabric.

12 POPPY
【Poppy Family】
Floral language: Comfort, Sympathy
**A charming flower with large airy petals.
Create them with bright orange and
yellow cotton or organdy in matching
shades.**

25

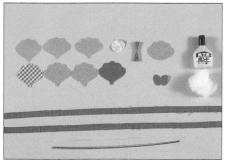

Materials per Flower and Bud:
Petals/Bud : 4" x 4" solid color cotton (A)
8" x 4" small-scale patterned cotton (B)
4" x 4" large scale patterned cotton (C)
8" x 4" organdy (D)
Center of flower : 2" x 2" cotton (E)
Stems/Calyx : 2" x 22" cotton (F)
4 14"-long #26 green stem wires, 1 #30
white stem wire, 60 2"-long stamens, Polyfil,
Craft glue

Make Flower

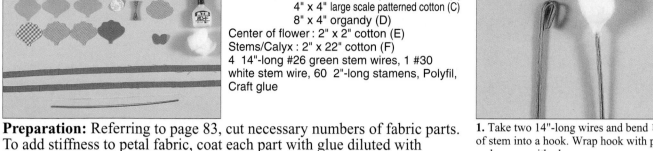

Preparation: Referring to page 83, cut necessary numbers of fabric parts. To add stiffness to petal fabric, coat each part with glue diluted with double amount of water, then let dry completely. Color stamens with yellow, orange, and yellowish green colored pencils.

1. Take two 14"-long wires and bend 1/4" end of stem into a hook. Wrap hook with polyfil, and secure with glue

2. Stitch around the center of flower fabric, 1/4" from raw edges. Leave thread attached.

3. Cover polyfil with fabric for flower center. Pull thread to gather fabric and slipstitch to secure.

4. Spread stamens on a flat surface and apply glue at 1/2" from each end so they stick together.

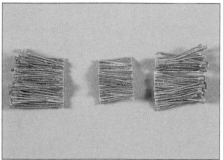

5. When the glue is still moist, cut stamens at 3/4" inside of each end.

6. Surround center of flower with the cut stamens and glue. Lightly curl stamens outwards.

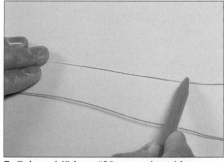

7. Color a 14"-long #30 stem wire with a colored pencil in the same shade as petal fabric. Cut the colored wire into 7 pieces, 2"-long each.

8. Dampen petal fabric with water.

9. Fold petal in half then twist tightly. Lightly unfold and let dry.

10. When dry, smooth petal with fingers, working from center toward the edge, to give it a shallow cup form.

11. Attach and glue a piece of the colored wire to the back of petal, 1" from top edge. Make 7 petals.

12. Attach petal to the underside of stamens.

13. Attach all 7 petals, sliding each so that they overlap evenly.

Make Stem

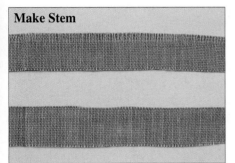

14. Make a shaggy stem fabric by gently pulling 2 or 3 weft threads from one side of the fabric.

15. Use shaggy side up to wrap the stem wire, starting at the base of petals, and apply glue as you work.

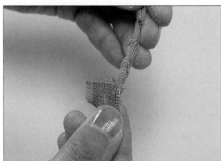

16. When the end of stem wire is reached, fold fabric upward and glue to secure.

Make Bud

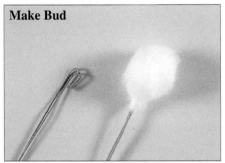

17. Take two 14"-long, #26 stem wires and bend 1/4" end of stem into a hook. Wrap polyfil around the hook and secure with glue.

18. Follow Steps 8-10 to make a petal. Wrap petal around polyfil.

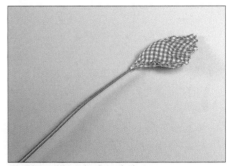

19. Shape like a bud, and glue to secure.

Make Stem for Bud

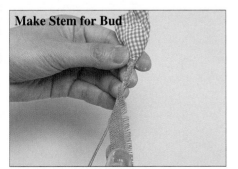

20. Prepare stem fabric in the same manner as in Step 14. With shaggy side up, wrap bud stem, starting below the bud.

21. Wrap the base of bud with calyx fabric. Glue to secure.

Completion

22. Adapt by changing color and pattern of petals.

13 LILY OF THE VALLEY

【Lily Family】

Floral language: Innocence, Subtlety

Attractive flower with multiple bell-shaped florets. Makes a dainty and exquisite nosegay. A perfect present.

Fabric Materials per Stem:
Petals : 6" x 4" cotton lace
Leaf : 6" x 10" cotton

Preparation: Referring to page 84, cut necessary numbers of fabric and other parts.

To assemble, you will need: 4" x 10" quilt batting, 5 #26 green stem wires, Polyfil, Green floral tape, Embroidery floss, Craft glue

Make Florets

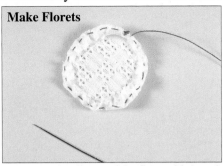

1. Turn in 1/8" all around the flower fabric and stitch 1/16" inside of the fold. Leave thread attached.

2. Lightly pull thread to gather and fill the hollow with polyfil.

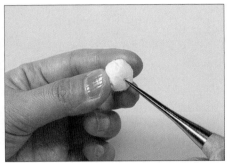

3. Using an awl, make a hole in the middle of the floret.

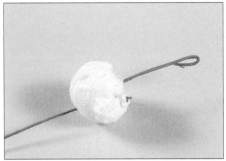

4. Cut stem wire into 6" and bend top part 1/4" into a loop. Insert unbent end of wire through the hole made in the flower. Place some glue on polyfil to secure wire.

5. Wind the upper part of wire around a pencil to curl. Make one large, two medium, and two small florets.

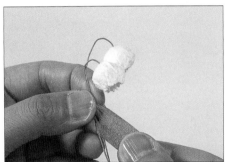

6. Assemble florets with floral tape. Start with 2 small florets, 3/4" apart, then attach 2 medium florets, 3/4" apart, and lastly attach the large floret.

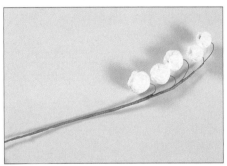

7. Flower stem completed. Make 2.

Make Leaf

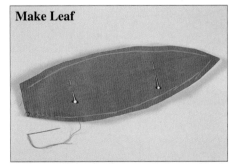

8. Layer quilt batting between 2 pieces of leaf fabric, right sides facing in, and stitch around through all three layers, 1/8" inside the raw edges. Leave opening unstitched.

9. Turn the fabric right side out. Slipstich to close opening. Stich veins of leaf with 2 strands of embroidery floss.

Attach Leaf

10. Wrap the two stems of flower with the leaf. Slipstich the base of leaf to secure. Tuck in excess wire.

Completion

11. Change size to use as a corsage.

●For easy comprehension, threads are shown in contrasting colors. When making actual projects, select matching shades for each fabric.

14 CALLA LILY

【Aroid Family】

Floral language: Love

The white and yellow flowers with long, slender stem really stand out in any setting. Enjoy combinations of colors and/or prints.

Fabric Materials per Stem:
Petal : 8" x 8" solid color fabric (A)
        8" x 8" printed fabric (B)
Center of flower : 2" x 4" toweling
Stem : 22" x 22" solid color fabric

Preparation: Referring to page 85, cut necessary numbers of fabric and other parts.

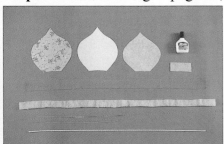

To assemble, you will need: 8" x 8" adhesive interlining, 1" x 27" batting strip, 1 extra-thick stem wire(1/4"), 2 #28 white stem wires, Craft glue

Make Petal

1. Attach adhesive interlining to the back of fabric B.

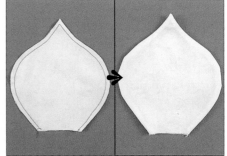

2. Layer fabric A and fabric B, right sides facing, and stitch together approx. 1/4" inside to outline interlining. Leave opening unstitched. Turn petal right side out and straighten shape. Turn in the raw edge of the opening.

3. Join tips of two #28 wires by twisting together. Shape wire to match the petal. Apply glue and insert into petal. Press edges to secure.

Make Stem

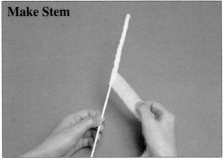

4. Place a line of glue along the length of extra-thick stem wire. Wrap wire with batting strip.

5. Turn in 3/8" along one side of stem fabric. Place wire on the fabric, leaving out 3" of wire, and slipstich to join raw edge of stem fabric to quilt batting. Stitch up to top of wire.

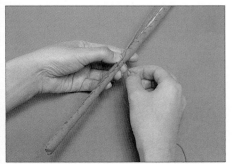

6. Fold in the bottom edge of stem fabric to cover stem end. Wrap stem with fabric to cover the stitches and slipstich along the folded crease in the other direction.

Make Flower

7. Fold center of flower fabric in half, right sides facing in. Stitch roundly along the marked line. Turn fabric right side out.

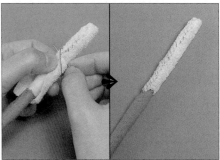

8. Place the center of flower fabric on the uncovered end of stem. Wrap stem with fabric and slipstich to secure.

9. Cut the petal wires leaving about 2", and twist them around the base of the flower center. Wrap petal around stem and slipstich to attach the opening of petal to stem.

10. Overlap the sides of petal to cover wires. Slipstich petal for 3/8" from the bottom of flower upward to secure.

Completion

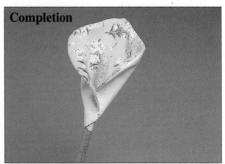

11. The printed side shows inside in this type. Enjoy variations.

●For easy comprehension, threads are shown in contrasting colors. When making actual projects, select matching shades for each fabric.

15 CALLA LILY

【Aroid Family】
Floral language: Majestic beauty, Maiden's gracefulness
The white flower with long, slender stem really stands out. Elegant and sophisticated when made with shiny satin fabric.

Fabric Materials per Stem:
Petal : 12" x 6" satin
Center of flower : 2" x 4" cotton
Stem : 20" x 2" cotton

Preparation: Referring to page 86, cut necessary numbers of fabric and other parts.

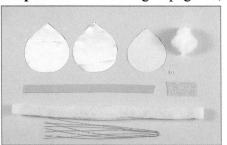

To assemble, you will need: 1" x 1 yd quilt strip, 6" x 6" adhesive interlining, 4 1 yd-long #22 bare stem wires, 1 3/8"-diam. button with 4 holes, Polyfil

Make Stem

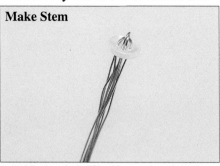

1. Fold wires in half and insert them into the button holes, 2 wires per hole.

2. Wrap the wire tightly with batting strip.

Make Center of Flower

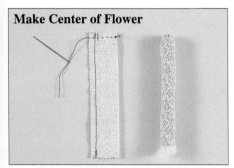

3. Fold fabric lengthwise in half, right sides facing in. Stitch along the side, 1/4" inside. Stitch the top, 1/4" inside, and pull thread to gather. Knot off. Turn the fabric right side out, and stuff the tube with polyfil.

4. Insert button end of wrapped stem wire into the center of flower.

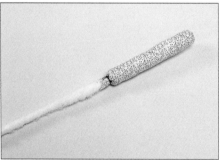

5. Tie the base with thread.

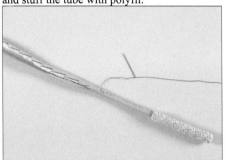

6. Wrap the wire with stem fabric and slipstich to secure.

Make Flower

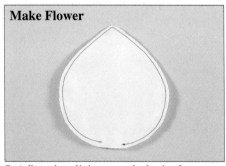

7. Adhere interlining onto the back of one petal fabric. Layer another petal fabric, right sides facing, and stitch together, 1/4" from raw edges. Leave opening unstitched. Turn petal right side out. Slipstitch to close opening.

Completion

8. Place petal at the base of the center of flower and stitch to secure.

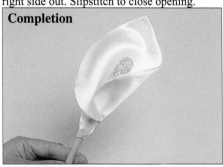

9. Curl petal outward and arrange the shape.

16 EASTER LILY

【Lily Family】

Floral language: Innocence

This graceful and beautiful plant bears several flowers that bloom sideways, so that even a single stem makes its presence strongly felt. Use pure white fabric to enhance its elegance.

Preparation: Referring to page 87, cut necessary numbers of fabric parts.

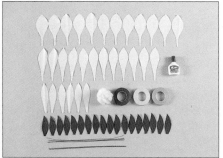

To assemble, you will need: 3 #28 green stem wires, 19 #26 stem wires, 2 #16 stem wires, Polyfil, Floral tapes (green, yellow, light brown), Craft glue

Make Petals

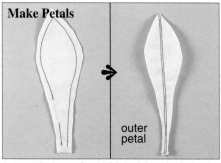

outer petal

1. Layer 2 pieces of petal fabric right sides facing in, and stitch together 1/4" inside. Leave opening unstitched. Turn petal right side out. Machine-stitch lengthwise 2 lines along the center, 1/10" apart.

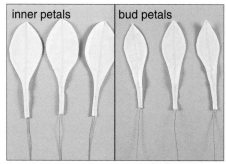

inner petals   bud petals

2. Insert a #26 stem wire through the gap between the machine-stitched lines. In the same manner, prepare 3 outer petals, 3 inner petals and 3 bud petals.

Make Pistils

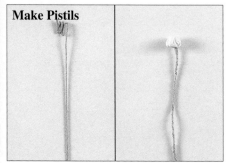

3. Coil an end of #26 wire, flatten it widthwise, and wrap it with yellow floral tape. Wrap the remaining part of wire with light brown floral tape for 6". Make 2.

Make Stamens

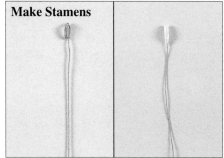

4. Bend an end of #28 wire, flatten it lengthwise, and wrap it with yellow floral tape. Make 12.

Make Flower

4"

5. Assemble 6 stamens to surround pistil. Allow 4" from the stamens, wrap the wires with green floral tape. Arrange three inner petals around this and wrap with green floral tape.

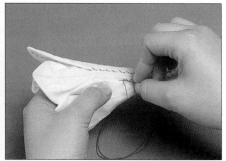

6. Stitch to attach the outer petal edges 1/4" beside the machine-stitched line of inner petals. Leave the upper 1/3 of petal unstitched.

7. Wrap the stem with floral tape, starting at the base of the outer petal.

Make Bud

8. Insert a #26 wire through the gap between the machine-stitched lines of bud fabric. Prepare 3 buds likewise. Butting 2 bud petals together, stitch edge to edge.

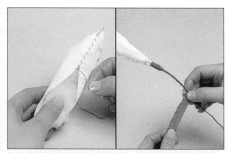

9. Join the third bud petal and stitch along the edge, stuffing with polyfil as you work. Tape down, starting at the base of the bud.

Make Leaves

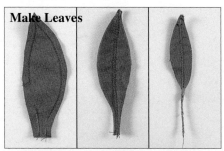

10. Layer 2 pieces of leaf fabric, right sides facing, and stitch together, 1/4" inside. Leave opening unstitched. Turn right side out . Machine-stitch 2 lines along the center, 1/10" apart. Insert a #26 wire between the gap. Wrap wire with floral tape.

Completion

11. Attach 2 flowers, 1 bud, and then 9 leaves around two #16 stem wires, and wrap with green floral tape for a finished stem of lily.

●For easy comprehension, threads are shown in contrasting colors. When making actual projects, select matching shades for each fabric.

Fabric Materials per Stem:
Petals: 12" x 6" light pink cotton (A)
6" x 6" pink cotton (B)
6" x 6" checked pattern cotton (C)
10" x 6" floral pattern cotton (D)
Leaf : 8" x 6" cotton (E)

17 HYDRANGEA
【Saxifrage Family】
Flower language: Capricious, You are cold
A flower that changes color while blooming. An ideal project to use scrap fabrics collected in purple, blue, and pink hues.

Preparation: Referring to page 88, cut necessary numbers of fabric parts.

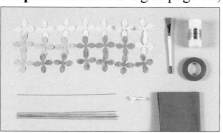

To assemble, you will need: 1 #20 green stem wire, 7 #26 green stem wires, Green floral tape, 21 stamens, Water-based varnish for decoupage finish

Make Florets

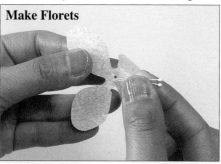

1. Make a hole in the middle of petal using an awl. Fold a stamen in half and insert it into the hole.

2. Cut a #26 stem wire into 3 1/2" length, and twist it around the base of petals.

3. Wrap the base of this floret and wire with floral tape. Make 21 florets.

4. Coat petals with water-based varnish and let dry.

5. Assemble 7 florets together and secure with floral tape. Make 3 clusters of florets.

6. Assemble the 3 clusters of florets around a 14"-long #20 stem wire and twist together all wires.

Make Leaf

7. Place leaf fabric right side up and transfer leaf motif from pattern onto it. Machine-stitch along the marking.

8. Cut along the outline of leaf with pinking shears. Gather the base of the leaf and secure it with a 7"-long #26 stem wire, folded in half. Wrap the base of the leaf with floral tape.

9. Coat leaf with water-based varnish and let dry. Double-coat the lower part of leaf with varnish, and let dry.

Attach Leaf

10. Start wrapping the flower stem with floral tape, 1" from the base of florets. Wrap 2" then attach leaf. Keep wrapping to the end of the wire.

Completion

11. Change colors and patterns of flower fabric to suit your taste.

●For easy comprehension, threads are shown in contrasting colors. When making actual projects, select matching shades for each fabric.

18 SUNFLOWER

【Chrysanthemum Family】
Floral language: You are wonderful

The bright yellow petals look like the sun itself. Create the tight buds and the flowers as if they just came into blossom. Arrange them freely in a large vases that will enhance their vivid look of the flowers.

Fabric Materials per Flower and Bud:
Petals/Bud : 18" x 4" yellow cotton (A)
                    8" x 4" yellow checked pattern cotton (B)
Center of flower : 6" x 6" brown toweling
Center for bud : 4" x 4" green toweling
Leaves/Calyxes : 1.2 yds x 6" green cotton

Preparation: Referring to page 89, cut necessary numbers of fabric and other parts.

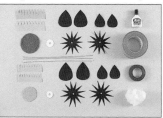

To assemble, you will need:
4" x 2" cardboard, 2 extra-thick stem wires(1/4"), 2 #26 stem wires, Polyfil, 2"-wide packing tape, Green floral tape, Craft glue

Stiffen Fabrics

1. Use a brush to coat petal fabric and calyx fabric with glue diluted with double amount of water.

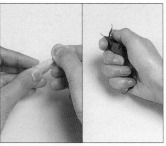

2. Wring petal fabric tightly while still damp to form creases and let dry. Squeeze calyx fabric while still damp to form creases and let dry.

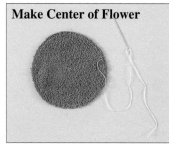

Make Center of Flower

3. Sew a tight running stitch around the rim of the center of flower fabric, 1/4" inside the edge. Leave thread attached.

4. Place polyfil in the hollow, and pull thread lightly until the opening is about 3/8" in diameter. The process will be easier if fabric is placed on a 1 3/4" to 2" diameter lid of a jar. Stuff polyfil firmly so the circumference measures 6".

5. Place some glue on cardboard. Attach cardboard to center of flower, matching the holes.

Attach Petals

6. Place a line of glue along the lower part of solid color petal and attach it to the center of flower. Place glue along the lower part of the patterned petal and attach it around the solid color petal, so the points of the petals are staggered.

Attach Calyx   (back)

7. Apply glue on the cardboard of the center of flower and around the lower part of petals (3/8" from bottom edge) to attach calyx, matching the holes. Attach the second calyx likewise so the points of the calyx are staggered.

Make Bud

8. Make the bud following the instructions for the flower. Coat the bud with glue diluted with water and lightly squeeze it with your hand. Let dry.

Make Leaves

9. Take one piece of leaf fabric (right side down) and apply some glue on the surface. Place a #26 stem wire in the middle of the fabric and layer another piece of leaf fabric, right side up.

10. After glue has dried, create creases by crumpling the fabric. Wrap floral tape holding at right angle under the base of the leaf only 2 to 3 times.

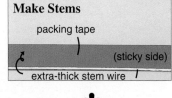

Make Stems

packing tape

(sticky side)

extra-thick stem wire

11. Cut 32" to 42" of extra-thick stem wire. Layer the same lengths of packing tape, sticky side up. Roll up tape around the wire to thicken.

12. Wrap the thickened stem entirely with floral tape.

13. Attach leaves to stem as desired, securing with floral tape.

14. Place some glue on the top of the stem and insert it into the bottom of the flower. Make bud in the same manner.

Completion

15. Open out the petals of the flower slightly.

Fabric Materials per Stem:
Large petal : 10" x 10" yellow cotton
Small petal : 8" x 8" orange cotton
Center of flower A : 6" x 6" printed cotton
Center of flower B : 32" x 4" brown cotton
Leaves/Stem/Calyx : 22" x 14" green cotton

19 SUNFLOWER
【Chrysanthemum Family】
Floral language: Big smile
**Large sunflowers that brightly bloom
under the summer sun. Their cheery
look will boost your spirits. Arrange
them nonchalantly in a large basket.**

40

Preparation: Referring to page 90, cut necessary numbers of fabric parts.

To assemble, you will need:
1" x 1 yd batting strip, Polyfil, 4 1 yd-long #22 bare stem wires, 4 7"-long #22 bare stem wires, 1 3/8"-diam. button with 4 holes, Craft glue

Make Stem

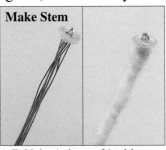

1. Fold the 4 pieces of 1 yd-long wires in half, and insert them into the button holes, 2 wires per hole. Wrap wires tightly with batting strip.

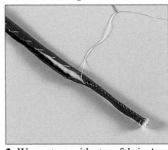

2. Wrap stem with stem fabric A and slipstitch to secure.

Make Center of Flower

3. Stitch around the rim of flower center fabric, 1/4" inside. Leave thread attached. Pull thread lightly and stuff hollow with polyfil firmly. Pull thread again to gather fabric. Knot off. Throw thread across the length and width of the opening several times to secure.

4. Fold the center of flower fabric B lengthwise in half. Make 3/8"-deep slits at 1/4" intervals into the fold. Attach this around the stuffed center A and stitch to secure.

5. Completed center of flower.

Make Flower

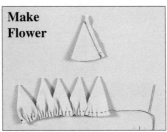

6. Fold one large petal fabric (yellow) in half, right sides facing in, and stitch along straight edge, 1/8" inside. Turn right side out. Make 16 petals. Stitch all petals in a row, 1/8" inside the bottom edge. Prepare small petals (orange) in the same manner.

7. Attach small petals around the center of flower and stitch to secure. Then attach large petals around the small petals. Stitch to secure.

8. Apply glue on the wired button, and insert it into the backside of stuffed center of flower. Stitch stem fabric to center of flower.

Make Calyx

9. Make 3/8"-long slits at 1/4" intervals around the rim of calyx A. Twist the fringes all around with your fingers. Turn in 1/4" all around calyx B and stitch along edges. Make matching tiny crisscross cut in the middle of each.

10. Insert stem through first calyx A then calyx B. Slipstitch around the edge of calyx B to secure it to the back of petals. Stitch stem to calyx B to secure.

Make Leaves

11. Stitch a pin tuck along the center-line of leaf. Repeat with all leaf fabric. Layer 2 pieces of tucked leaf fabric, and stitch all around, 1/4" inside. Leave opening unstitched. Snip small cuts around the edges and turn leaf inside out.

12. Machine-stitch the veins of leaf. Insert one 7"-long #22 stem wire through the tuck on each side.

13. Wrap leaf stem with quilt batting for about 4" from the top. Wrap with stem fabric B, and slipstitch to secure. Make 2.

Attach Leaves

14. Attach first leaf to the flower stem 4" below the base of flower. Stitch to secure. Stitch second leaf 2" below the first one. Starting from the underside of second leaf, wrap 12"-long batting strip around the stem. Cover with stem fabric C and slipstitch to secure.

Completion

15. Slightly bend the stem at the base of blossom and arrange shape.

●For easy comprehension, threads are shown in contrasting colors. When making actual projects, select matching shades for each fabric.

20 CLEMATIS
【Buttercup Family】
Floral language: Nobleness
A climber that grows on trellis. These striking deep purple blossoms feature Japanese clematis.

Fabric Materials per Stem:
Petals : 12" x 4" printed purple cotton
Center of flower : 4" x 2" brown printed
cotton
Leaves : 8" x 4" green cotton

42

Preparation: Referring to page 88, cut necessary numbers of fabric parts.

To assemble, you will need: 4 #24 stem wires, 6 #26 stem wires, Water-based matte varnish (used for finishing decoupage), Brush, Dark brown floral tape, Craft glue

Make Flower

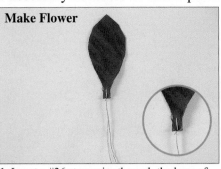

1. Insert a #26 stem wire through the base of the petal and fold wire in half. Twist wire to secure. Make 6 petals.

2. Using a brush, coat petals with water-based matte varnish to stiffen the fabric.

3. When varnish is dry, use a spatula or the edge of a ruler to mark three veins lengthwise.

Make Center of Flower

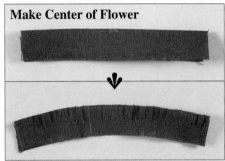

4. Fold flower center fabric lengthwise in half, wrong sides facing in. Make 1/8"-long slits 1/4" apart, into the fold.

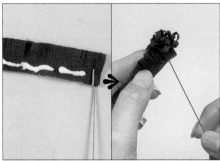

5. Place a line of glue along the edge of flower center fabric. Bend an end of #24 stem wire and hook it onto one of the slits. Wrap the fabric around the wire.

6. Using a pair of scissors, cut the loops just formed.

7. Attach the 6 petals around the center of flower and secure with floral tape.

Make Leaves

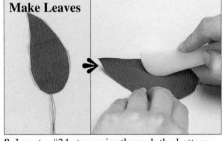

8. Insert a #24 stem wire through the bottom part of leaf fabric. Fold in half the wire and twist to secure. Using a brush, coat leaves with water-based matte varnish to stiffen fabric. When varnish is dry, use a spatula or the edge of a ruler to mark three veins lengthwise.

9. Wrap stem for leaves with floral tape. Make 3 stems of leaves.

Attach Leaves

10. Attach them together to the flower stem so they extend outward, and secure with floral tape.

Completion

11. Completed clematis vine. Join several if preferred.

●For easy comprehension, threads are shown in contrasting colors. When making actual projects, select matching shades for each fabric.

21 GLORY LILY
【Lily Family】
Floral language: Tenacity
An impressive flower with wavy, vibrant petals. Since it is a climber, enjoy a free and natural form when arranging.

Fabric Materials per Stem:
Petals : 4" x 1 yd printed cotton
Leaves : 10" x 8" solid color cotton

Preparation: Referring to page 91, cut necessary numbers of fabric parts.

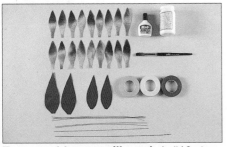

To assemble, you will need: 1 #16 stem wire, 4 #20 stem wires, 6 #26 stem wires, 8 #30 stem wires, Floral tapes (light brown, light green, green), Water-based matte varnish (used for finishing decoupage), Brush, Craft glue

Make Flower

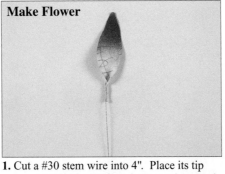

1. Cut a #30 stem wire into 4". Place its tip on a petal fabric, 1/2" from bottom edge. Apply glue and wrap the edges of petal around the wire.

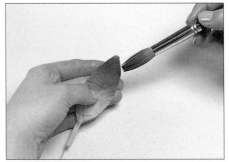

2. Coat petal with water-based matte varnish to stiffen fabric.

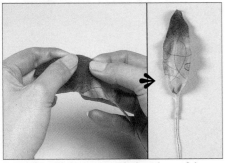

3. While still damp, stretch the edges of the petal to give it a wavy form. Fold the petal in half, wrong sides facing in, to crease the center line. Let dry.

Make Stamens

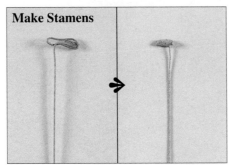

4. Wind 3/8" top part of #26 stem wire a couple of times, then flatten it crosswise. Wrap the top part of wire with light brown floral tape. Make 6 stamens.

Make Pistil

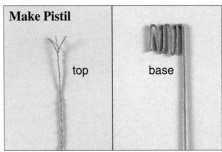

top   base

5. Assemble three #30 stem wires. Start twisting the three wires together, allowing 3/8" at top end and twist for 1". Take one #20 stem wire and bend the top end to shape three "waves," each 1/2" long as base.

6. Wrap light green floral tape around each "wave." Push the pistil wire through the center "wave." Pressing lower half of the "waves," wrap the lower floral tape.

Make Center of Flower

7. Attach the 6 stamens around the pistil and secure with floral tape.

Make Flower

8. Wrap the 6 petals around the center of flower and secure with green floral tape.

Make Leaves

9. Cut a #20 stem wire into 4". Place a line of glue on wire and attach it to bottom of the leaf. Wrap the edges of the leaf around the wire.

10. Follow the same procedure as for petals: Coat leaf with varnish to stiffen fabric. Let dry. Mark the veins of the leaf on the back of the fabric. Wrap the wire with floral tape.

Completion

11. Assemble 3 flowers and 4 leaves to a #16 stem wire securing with floral tape. Consider the balance of the whole stem as you assemble.

●For easy comprehension, threads are shown in contrasting colors. When making actual projects, select matching shades for each fabric.

Fabric Materials per Stem:
Petals : 4" x 1 yd solid color cotton
Leaves : 4" x 1.2 yds solid color cotton

22 GENTIAN
【Gentian Family】
Floral language: Justice

A beautiful and dignified flower found in fields, gently swaying in the autumnal breeze. The fabric used here is hand-dyed in purple, which gives more depth to the color. Impressive also when arranged in baskets.

46

Preparation: Referring to page 91, cut necessary numbers of fabric parts.

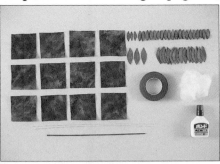

To assemble, you will need: 1 extra-thick stem wire (1/8"), 10 #22 stem wires, 4 #24 stem wires, Polyfil, Green floral tape, Craft glue

Make Florets

1. Cut a #24 stem wire into 4". Bend tip and hook it onto polyfil formed into a ball. Place petal fabric right side down. Fold the shorter edge in half, crosswise.

2. Fold in half again to crease center, and unfold. Fold in one corner of the doubled side toward the center crease to form a triangle. Fold the opposite corner toward the back-side in the same manner.

3. Insert the wire with polyfil in the pocket formed between the triangles.

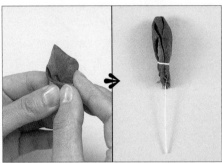

4. Fold one corner of the triangle to the front, and the other corner to the back to make an evenly ballooned floret. Secure the base tightly with thread. Make 12.

Make Leaves

5. Cut #22 stem wire into 2" (for large leaves) and 1" (for small leaves) pieces. Apply glue to the back of a leaf fabric and attach the stem wire which corresponds to the size.

6. Cover with another piece of leaf fabric. Make 10 large leaves and 48 small ones.

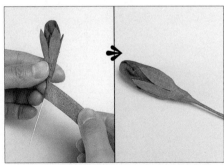

7. Attach 4 small leaves around petal and secure with thread. Start wrapping floral tape at 3/8" above the base of the floret. Make 12 of this floret.

8. Assemble 4 florets and start wrapping the stem at 2 1/4" below the base of florets. Make 3 of this unit.

9. Cut 14" out of extra-thick stem wire. Attach one flower unit at the top of wire and wrap with floral tape. Attach 2 large leaves below the flower and wrap for 3" with floral tape.

10. Repeat with the remaining units of flowers and leaves, allowing 3" between each. Attach remaining leaves in a balanced manner.

Completion

11. Natural looking stem of gentian completed.

●For easy comprehension, threads are shown in contrasting colors. When making actual projects, select matching shades for each fabric.

Fabric Materials per Stem:
Petals/Buds : 6" x 4" cotton
Leaves/Stems/Calyxes : 28" x 2" cotton
Center of flower : 4" x 3" light green cotton(A)
: 2" x 2" light blue cotton (B)

23 CHINESE BELLFLOWER
【Bellflower Family】
Floral language: Unchanging love, Integrity
These star-shaped petals and balloon-shaped buds are the characteristics of this flower which mark the arrival of autumn. Shading purple fabric creates an aura of quiet autumnal mellowness.

Preparation: Referring to page 92, cut necessary numbers of fabric parts. To add stiffness to petal, leaf, stem and calyx fabric, coat each part with glue diluted with double amount of water, then let dry completely.

To assemble, you will need:
1 14"-long #20 green stem wire, 4 #26 green stem wires, Polyfil, Craft glue

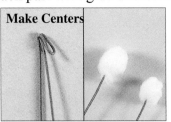

Make Centers

1. Bend a 14"-long #26 stem wire in half. Make a hook with 1/4" of bent tip and wrap polyfil around it to form a ball. Make 2 balls 1" in diameter (large center for buds) and 1 ball 1/2" in diameter (small center for flower).

2. Stitch around small center of flower fabric, 1/4" inside. Leave thread attached. Stuff it with polyfil, and pull thread to gather. Stitch to secure. Prepare 2 large centers likewise.

Make Flower and Buds

3. Join and glue the edges to form flower. Seam allowance should show outside.

4. Prepare small petals and calyxes likewise. Seam allowances should stay inside.

5. Place some glue on the underside of the small center of flower. Insert wire of small center of flower through large petal, and glue together.

6. Place some glue on the inner side of medium calyx. Insert large flower stem wire through it and glue together.

7. Assemble a small flower with a small center of flower and small calyx in the same manner.

8. Insert a large center through a small flower. Place some glue on the edges of the petal and pinch together the edges next to each other to close.

9. Place some glue inside a small calyx and attach it to the bud. Completed large bud.

10. Place some glue on the underside of a large center. Insert the large center of flower stem wire through a large calyx and glue together. Completed small bud.

Make Leaves

11. Cut out 2 1/4" pieces out of a #26 stem wire. Glue this wire to the back of a leaf fabric. Make 4 large leaves and 2 small leaves.

Attach Leaves

12. Start wrapping the stem of large petal with stem fabric, beneath the calyx. Apply glue to secure stem fabric. Attach 2 large leaves 1" below the calyx then wrap another 4".

13. Wrap stem of large bud with stem fabric, starting beneath the calyx. Apply glue to secure stem fabric. Attach 2 small leaves 1 1/2" below the calyx and wrap to the end of the wire. Wrap stem of small bud.

14. Attach large flower and large bud to #20 stem wire and wrap with stem fabric. Glue to secure. Attach small bud and 2 large leaves 4" below, and wrap with stem fabric to the end of wire.

Completion

15. Completed basic form. Adapt by changing color and pattern of flower, or the shape of stem.

●For easy comprehension, threads are shown in contrasting colors. When making actual projects, select matching shades for each fabric.

Fabric Materials per Stem:
Petals/Bud : 16" x 4" solid color cotton
Leaves/Calyxes : 20" x 6" solid color cotto

24 DIANTHUS

【Dianthus Family】

Floral language: Chastity

A flower with delicate fringed petals. Also called "Yamato Nadeshiko," which is a synonym for the ideal image of a Japanese woman. Use different shades of pink fabric to add expression to the flower.

Preparation: Referring to page 93, cut necessary numbers of fabric parts.

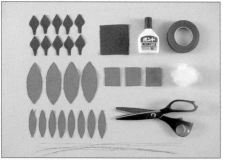

To assemble, you will need: 16 #28 stem wires, Polyfil, Green floral tape, Pinking shears, Craft glue

Make Flowers

1. Place a line of glue on top part of a #28 stem wire and attach it to backside of a petal, 3/4" below the top edge. Glue the lower sides of petal together, by wrapping around the wire.

2. Make fine slits all around the petal. Assemble 5 petals and twist the wires together.

3. Wrap 1 1/2"-length of stem with polyfil beneath the petals. Wind thread to secure.

Make Calyxes

4. Cut upper edge of calyx fabric with pinking shears. On the wrong side of fabric, apply glue below the zig-zag. Wrap this around the bound polyfil. Turn in side edge of fabric and slipstich to secure.

5. Wrap wire with floral tape, covering the bottom edge of the calyx. Make 2 of this stem.

Make Bud

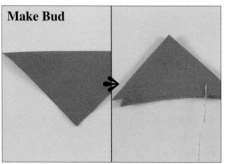

6. Fold bud fabric in half into a triangle. Fold in half again. Hook one end of wire into folded side, and twist the wire together.

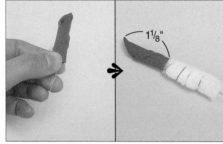

7. Place some glue along the bottom edge of fabric and roll fabric around the wire. Wrap 1 1/2"-length of stem with polyfil, 1 1/8" beneath the bottom edge of bud fabric. Wind thread to secure.

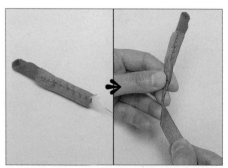

8. Refer to Step 4 to attach calyx to bud. Wrap wire with floral tape, covering the bottom edge of the calyx.

Make Leaves

9. Place some glue on the back of leaf fabric. Attach a #28 stem wire and cover with another piece of leaf fabric. Make 2 large leaves and 4 small ones.

10. Assemble 2 flowers and 2 small leaves and wrap with floral tape. Attach the bud and 2 small leaves below the flowers. Wrap with floral tape again and lastly attach 2 large leaves.

Completion

11. Tape down to the end of stem for finished dianthus.

●For easy comprehension, threads are shown in contrasting colors. When making actual projects, select matching shades for each fabric.   51

Fabric Materials per Stem:
Petals : 6" x 2" cotton
Center of flower : 10" x 2" cotton
Leaves/Stem : 24" x 4" cotton

25 COSMOS
【Chrysanthemum Family】
Floral language: Harmony, Wholeheartedness
A flower with simple beauty that inspires nostalgic memories. The sight of cosmos flowers swaying in the breeze is very pretty. Make a bunch of them with checked gingham and solid color cotton in assorted colors.

Preparation: Referring to page 93, cut necessary numbers of fabric parts. To add stiffness to fabric, coat each part with glue diluted with double amount of water then let dry completely.

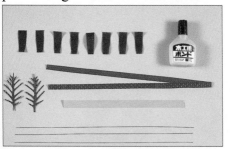

To assemble, you will need: 4 #26 stem wires, Craft glue

Make Center of Flower

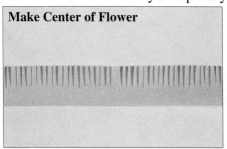

1. Make 1/4"-deep slits at 1/16" intervals on the flower center fabric.

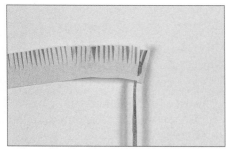

2. Assemble three 14"-long wires together, bend the top and hook them to a slit of the fabric.

3. Roll the fabric around the wires and secure the edge with glue.

Make Flower

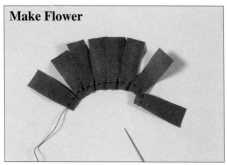

4. Stitch together 8 petal pieces in a row.

5. Join ends to make the petals into a circle. Leave thread attached.

6. Insert wire of flower center through the petal circle. Pull the thread to gather the petals. Arrange the shape of petals and wind the thread two times around the base. Knot off.

Make Leaves

7. Cut a #26 stem wire into 3" and attach to the back of a leaf with glue. Make 2 leaves.

8. Start wrapping the wire with stem fabric from beneath the base of flower, applying glue to secure fabric to stem.

Attach Leaves

9. Attach the two leaves at 1" intervals from the base of the flower. Wrap with stem fabric up to the end of the wire.

10. Trim the edge of petals with pinking shears.

Completion

11. Adapt by changing color and pattern of petals and leaves.

●For easy comprehension, threads are shown in contrasting colors. When making actual projects, select matching shades for each fabric.

26 GREAT BURNET

【Rose Family】

Floral language: As days go by

Flowers that brightly sway in the autumnal fields. Create them by rolling narrow strips of fringed fabric. Arrange them naturally.

Fabric Materials per Stem:
Petals : 2" x 2" wool (A)
         2" x 2" knitted wool (B)
         2" x 2" tartan plaid wool (C)
Leaves : 4" x 2" cotton

Preparation: Referring to page 94, cut necessary numbers of fabric parts.

To assemble, you will need:
1 green #20 stem wire, 4 green
#26 stem wires, Polyfil,
Craft glue, Green floral tape

Make Blossom

1. Cut a #26 stem wire into 7". Bend the top 1/4", wrap polyfil around it, and secure it with glue to resemble a cotton swab. Make 4 large and 3 small ones.

2. Make 1/8"-deep slits at 1/8" intervals into the long side of petal fabric.

3. Applying glue only to the bottom, wrap it around the polyfil at an angle, fringed side up. Cut off excess. Make 4 with fabric A, 2 with fabric B and 1 with fabric C. Vary the size as desired.

Make Leaves

4. Layer two pieces of leaf fabric right sides facing in, and stitch along the edges, 1/8" inside. Leave opening unstitched. Turn fabric right side out.

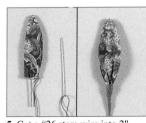

5. Cut a #26 stem wire into 2" and insert into the leaf. Gather-stitch to close opening around the wire. Pull thread and knot off. Wrap the base of leaf and the wire with floral tape. Make 2.

6. Attach 3 florets to the top of a 14"-long #20 stem wire. Wrap with floral tape to secure.

Attach Leaves

7. As you tape down, attach 2 florets about 3" below the first 3, then one floret and 2 leaves 3" below.

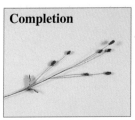

Completion

8. Adapt by changing the number of flowers and shape of stem.

●For easy comprehension, threads are shown in contrasting colors. When making actual projects, select matching shades for each fabric.

27 ALLIUM GIGANTEUM

【Lily Family】

Floral language: Right assertion

Hundreds of tiny petals densely bloom on a spherical head. Besides purple, they look nice in pale pink or pale blue fabric. Vary the height of stems so that they won't overlap.

Fabric Materials per Stem:
Petals: 8" x 1.2 yds printed cotton

Preparation: Referring to page 94, cut necessary numbers of fabric parts.

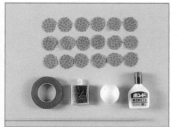

To assemble, you will need:
1 2"-diam. styrofoam ball, 1 1/4"-diam. 24"- long round wood stick, 120 setting pins, Green floral tape, Craft glue

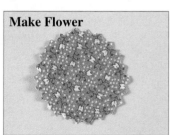

Make Flower

1. Trim the edge of petal fabric with pinking shears.

2. Fold petal fabric in half, wrong sides facing in, then fold in half again.

3. Fold one of the ears in half toward the edge. Fold one ear to front, the other to back.

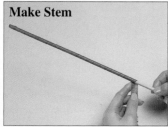

Make Stem

4. Wrap the round wood stick with floral tape.

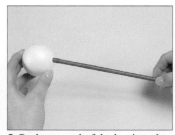

5. Push one end of the bar into the styrofoam sphere and glue to secure.

6. Insert a setting pin in the folds of petal and push the pin into the styrofoam. Start from the top of the sphere and fill in gaps densely.

Completion

7. Trim the surface with pinking shears to smooth out the sphere for finished allium.

●For easy comprehension, threads are shown in contrasting colors. When making actual projects, select matching shades for each fabric.

Fabric Materials per Stem:
Outer petal : 12" x 4" light purple cotton
Inner petals/Bud : 10" x 2" purple cotton
Leaves : 6" x 4" green felt
Calyx for flower : 4" x 2" green cotton
Calyx for bud : 2" x 2" yellow cotton

28 CORNFLOWER
【Chrysanthemum Family】
Floral language: Delicacy, Elegance
**This flower comes in many
refreshing colors, such as white,
pink, blue, and purple. A calming
effect is achieved by the innocent
look of these wild flowers.**

Preparation: Referring to page 94, cut necessary numbers of fabric parts. To add stiffness to petal fabric, coat each part with glue diluted with double amount of water then let dry completely.

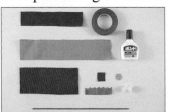

To assemble, you will need:
1 extra-thick stem wire(1/8"), 1 #24 stem wire, Polyfil, Green floral tape, Craft glue

Make Flower

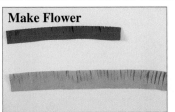

1. Fold outer petal fabric lengthwise in half wrong sides facing in. Make 3/4"-deep slits along the fold at 1/4" intervals. For the inner petal fabric, make 3/8"-deep slits at 1/4" intervals.

2. Using glue, attach the extra-thick stem wire to one edge of the inner petal fabric.

3. Wind the inner petal fabric tightly around the wire.

4. Tightly bind the base of petals with thread.

5. Likewise, securely wind the outer petal fabric around the inner petals, aligning bottom lines of both fabrics. Wind thread tightly to secure.

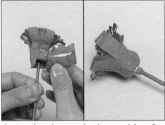

6. Apply glue to the inner side of the calyx fabric and wrap it around of the outer petals covering the thread. Gather the lower part of calyx fabric around the stem and bind with thread.

Add Movement to Petals

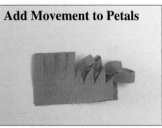

7. To add movement to the petals, to the petals turning inside out the loops of the outer row and innermost row of fabric as shown.

Make Bud

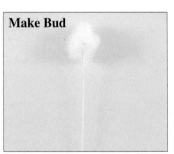

8. Cut a 4" piece out of a #24 stem wire. Bend one end and wrap some polyfil around it.

9. Cover the polyfil with bud fabric and bind the base with thread to secure.

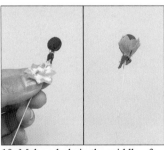

10. Make a hole in the middle of bud calyx fabric. Place some glue on the fabric. Insert bud wire through the hole and attach calyx to the underside of bud.

Make Leaves

11. Stiffen leaf fabric with laundry starch. Cut a strip of 3", and cut narrow, 1/4"-wide triangles across the width, alternating direction at each cut. Make about 45 to 50 leaves.

12. Cut a 6" piece out of a #24 stem wire. Attach 15 leaves around wire with floral tape. Arrange into a shapely form for a finished leaf stem.

13. Attach 7 leaves to the bud stem by wrapping downward with floral tape from the bud.

14. Attach blossom to craft wire by wrapping with floral tape. Add bud stem and remaining leaves 2 1/4" interval, and then add the leaf stems in sequence.

Completion

15. Adapt by changing colors of blossom.

● For easy comprehension, threads are shown in contrasting colors. When making actual projects, select matching shades for each fabric.

Fabric Materials per Stem:
Leaves : 24" x 4" solid color cotton

29 GOLDEN MIMOSA
【Pulse Family】
Floral language: Sensitive mind
**The impression of mimosa branches laden with
"golden bonbons", gloriously blooming under
the spring sun, is pleasantly re-created with fluffy
wool yarn in bright yellow.**

Preparation: Referring to page 94 cut necessary numbers of fabric parts.

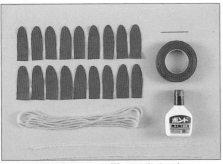

To assemble, you will need: 2 yds chunky wool yarn(yellow), 1 #20 stem wire, 4 #28 stem wires, Green floral tape, Wool needle, Craft glue

Make Blossoms

1. Thread wool needle with wool yarn. Place the needle in the middle of yarn. Wind the right-side yarn 5 times around the needle.

2. Pull the needle through the loops of yarn to make a loose rosette.

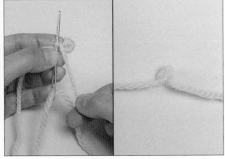

3. Place the needle next to the rosette, wind yarn one time around the needle. Pull the needle to form a knot.

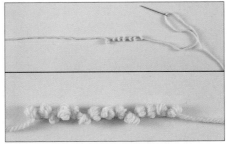

4. Repeat the Steps 1 to 3 and make 7 continuous knots toward the right. Go back to the middle of the yarn and this time, make knots with the left-side yarn. Make 7 knots on the left. Trim ends.

Make Stem

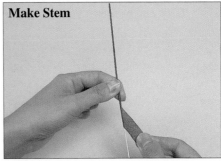

5. Wrap floral tape along a #20 stem wire.

6. Place some glue on the tip of the stem wire. Wrap the wire with the knotted wool. Glue top and bottom of the florets to secure.

Make Leaves

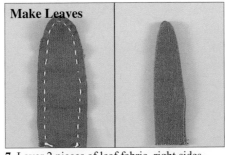

7. Layer 2 pieces of leaf fabric, right sides facing in, and stitch along the edges leaving 1/4" seam allowance. Leave opening unstitched. Turn fabric right side out and press with an iron.

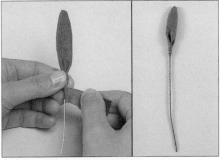

8. Cut a #28 stem wire into 5" , and insert it into the leaf. Wrap with floral tape. Make 6. In the same manner, make 3 leaves with 7"- long wire.

9. Attach two short leaves to a long one and secure with floral tape. Make 3 of this unit.

10. Attach the leaves to flower stem with floral tape.

Completion

11. Finished stem of mimosa.

●For easy comprehension, threads are shown in contrasting colors. When making actual projects, select matching shades for each fabric.

Fabric Materials per Stem:
Center of flower : 4" x 2" red solid color cotton (A)
Bracts : 14" x 6" red solid color cotton (B)
　　　　 8" x 6" red polka dot cotton (C)
　　　　 6" x 6" red checked pattern cotton (D)
　　　　 18" x 8" green solid color cotton (E)
　　　　 8" x 4" green checked pattern cotton (F)
Stem : 10" x 2" green solid color cotton (G)

30 POINSETTIA
【Spurge Family】
Floral language: Blessing, My heart is afire
A flower which can't be missed on Christmas. The bracts are made with red and green fabric and the yellow flowers with embroidery floss.

Preparation: Referring to page 95, cut necessary numbers of fabric parts.

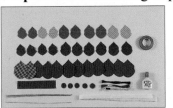

To assemble, you will need:
1" x 1 yd batting strip, 1 # 20 green stem wire, 7 #26 green stem wires, Green floral tape, Embroidery floss (red, yellow, green), Craft glue

Make Center of Flower

1. Cut a #26 stem wire into 2¼" and bend ¼" of one end. Assemble 8 pieces of embroidery floss cut into 1½" length. Fold them in half and hook the bent tip of wire in the fold. Twist wires tightly to secure.

2. Turn in ⅛" around center of flower fabric and stitch along edges. Leave thread attached.

3. Using an awl, make a hole in the middle of the flower fabric. Insert the wire of flower center through the hole.

4. Cover twisted wire with flower center fabric. Pull the hanging thread to gather and stitch to secure. Make 5 in the same manner.

Make Bract

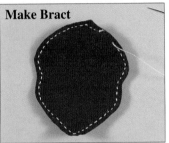

5. Layer 2 pieces of bract fabric, right sides facing in, and stitch along edges leaving ⅛" seam allowance. Leave opening unstitched.

6. Turn bract fabric right side out, slipstitch to close opening, and stitch to draw bract veins with embroidery thread.

7. Cut #26 stem wire into 5". Insert wire into bract and glue to secure. Make 6 large bracts, 6 medium bracts and 4 small ones.

8. Assemble 3 centers of flower and attach to a #20 stem wire with floral tape. Cut off excess wire of flower centers.

9. Attach 4 small bracts by wrapping with floral tape.

10. Attach 6 medium bracts by wrapping with floral tape.

11. Attach 4 large bracts (green) and secure with floral tape.

Make Stem

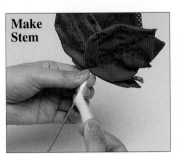

12. Wrap batting strip downward, around the wire from beneath the green bracts thickly layering over the previous wrap.

13. Wrap with the stem fabric and slipstich to secure, turning edges inside.

14. Insert 2 large leaves below the bracts and glue to secure.

Completion

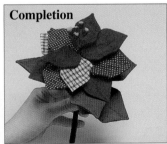

15. Adapt by changing colors and patterns of bracts.

● For easy comprehension, threads are shown in contrasting colors. When making actual projects, select matching shades for each fabric.

61

31 DAFFODIL

【Amaryllis Family】

Floral language: Integrity, Narcissism

A gentle flower that blooms in the bright spring sunshine. Here is a trumpet daffodil, made from white and yellow cotton.

Fabric Materials per Stem:
Outer petals : 12" x 6" white cotton
Bell petal : 8" x 4" yellow cotton
Leaves/Stem : 4" x 10" yellowish green cotton
Bract : 6" x 4" olive green cotton

Preparation: Referring to page 95, cut necessary numbers of fabric parts.

To assemble, you will need: 1" x 24" batting strip, 2 18"- lengths and 4 24"-lengths #22 stem wires, 5 stamens, 1 3/8"-diam. button with 4 holes, Craft glue

Make Stem

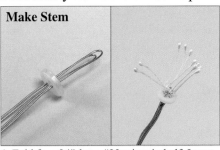

1. Fold four 24"-long #22 wires in half. Insert 4 ends of wire into two button holes, 2 ends per hole. Fold stamens in half and catch them in the wire loops. Insert remaining wires into the remaining button holes.

2. Wrap the wire tightly with batting strip from beneath the button. Secure beginning and end with glue.

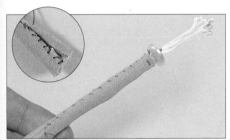

3. Attach stem fabric to wire. Baste one edge of fabric to the wrapped batting, then wrap the remaining fabric around stem and slipstich to secure, tucking in the edge and end of fabric.

Make Flower

4. Fold bell petal fabric lengthwise in half, wrong sides facing in. Make 1/4"-deep slits along the fold at 1/4" intervals. Wrap it around the stem two times and secure ends with glue. Bind the base tightly with thread.

5. Fold outer petal fabric in half and stitch along the seam edge, 5mm inside. Turn right side out. Make 6 petals. Join 3 petals by stitching them together. Leave thread attached. Make 2 of this unit.

6. Wrap one unit of outer petals around the bell petal. Pull the thread to gather fabric and stitch to secure. Attach the other outer petal unit in the same manner so that petals do not overlap.

Make Bract

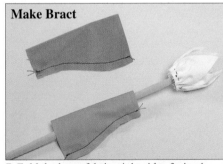

7. Fold the bract fabric, right sides facing in, and stitch along the side edge 1/4" inside. Leave thread attached. Insert the flower stem through it, narrow end up.

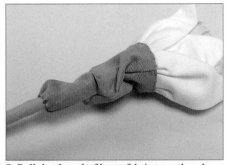

8. Pull the thread of bract fabric to gather the fabric, and knot off. Turn bract fabric upward. Slightly slack off fabric and slipstich both fabric ends to secure.

Make Leaves

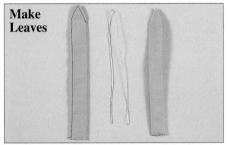

9. Fold a leaf fabric right sides facing in, and stitch along the edges, 1/4" inside. Leave opening unstitched. Turn fabric right side out. Insert a 18" long wire folded in half. Slipstich to close opening. Make 2 leaves.

Attach Leaves

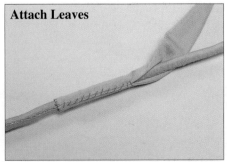

10. Wrap first leaf around stem and slipstich to secure. Place the second leaf about 2" below the first one and slipstich to secure.

Completion

11. Slightly bend the head of the flower at an angle and open up the leaves for completed daffodil.

●For easy comprehension, threads are shown in contrasting colors. When making actual projects, select matching shades for each fabric.

32 FRAMED TULIPS

A kitten napping in the warmth of sunshine filtering through the window and tulips nodding in the breeze. This is a pretty 3-D picture portraying a casual sketch of everyday life.

◆ Instructions on page 96

33 FRAMED HYDRANGEAS

This is a framed picture of hydrangeas and leaves arranged into a wreath. Clear beads on the leaves look like raindrops, and the little girl with an umbrella portray a rainy day.

◆ Instructions on page 98

34 BASKET OF WILD ROSES

Freshly picked wild roses brim over the basket. A curious mouse is tempted out of the hole by the fragrance of the roses, and here comes Mick, the black cat, tired of napping. A small afternoon scene depicted in a frame.

◆ Instructions on page 100

35 AUTUMN FLOWERS AT A MOONLIGHT PARTY

Tonight is the Moonlight Party to view the round full moon. The hares from the woods look happy. The silver grass and asters gently rustle in the autumnal breeze, glowing in the moonlight.

◆ Instructions on page 102

36 RUDBECKIAS SWAYING IN THE BREEZE

Sketch one of your fondest memories like this one, lovely yellow rudbeckias swaying in the breeze while you enjoy reading under a clear summer sky.

◆ Instructions on page 104

37   SONG OF PASSIFLORA

Passiflora, or passion flower, warms your heart with wide-open blossoms bathing in the sun. Do you hear the bird humming?

◆ Instructions on page 106

38/39   ROSE TOPIARY

Topiaries are plants trimmed into specific shapes. These large and small rose topiaries can easily be made with rolled fabric pieces, and yet they are stunningly showy.

◆ Instructions on page 114

40   ROSE BALLOON WITH BASKET

This rose balloon will cheer up any corner of your room. A tiny teddy bear is the passenger of this hot-air trip.

◆ Instructions on page 110

38

39

41   SMALL ROSE BOX

This small hat box is entirely covered with fabric and the lid is decorated with rolled fabric roses and white lace. A box where you may want to keep your favorite jewelry.

◆ Instructions on page 109

42 RED PEPPER WREATH

A cute arrangement of plump red peppers and round holly berries, accented with gold ribbons.

◆ Instructions on page 70

43 GRAPE WREATH

A wreath adorned with grape clusters of muted shades. Attach the fruit in a balanced manner.

◆ Instructions on page 112

Materials

Peppers/Berries : 6" x 6" solid red cotton (A)
                   6" x 6" polka dot pattern cotton (B)
                   6" x 6" checked pattern cotton (C)
Leaves/Calyxes : 12" x 4" solid green cotton (D)
Wreath base   : 1 ft x 2" solid brown cotton (E)

Preparation: Cut necessary numbers of fabric parts.

2" x 3.8 yds quilt batting, 9 14"-long #20 green stem wires, 8 14"-long #26 green stem wires, 1.7 yds 1/2"-wide ribbon, Craft glue, Polyfil, Embroidery floss

ACTUAL-SIZE PATTERNS
☆ Seam allowance included.

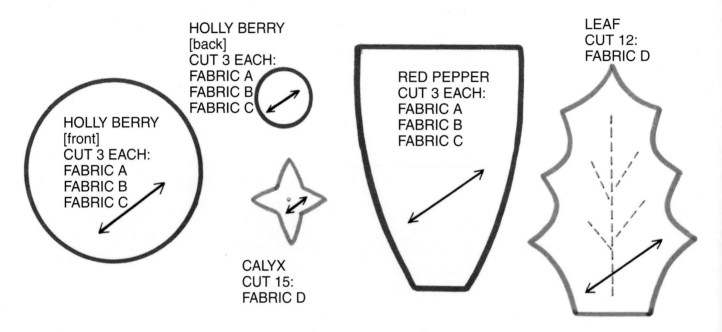

HOLLY BERRY
[back]
CUT 3 EACH:
FABRIC A
FABRIC B
FABRIC C

HOLLY BERRY
[front]
CUT 3 EACH:
FABRIC A
FABRIC B
FABRIC C

CALYX
CUT 15:
FABRIC D

RED PEPPER
CUT 3 EACH:
FABRIC A
FABRIC B
FABRIC C

LEAF
CUT 12:
FABRIC D

Make Wreath Base

2 1/2"   2 1/2"

1. Make a 1 yd-long wire rope by assembling 9 pieces of #20 stem wire, winding each around and staggering 2 1/2" with each wire. Twist together.

2. Form a ring of 7"-in diameter. Wind both ends to blend with the rest of the wires.

3. Completed ring.

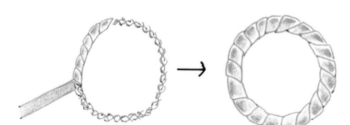

4. Wrap quilt batting around the ring two times to add thickness, and glue both ends.

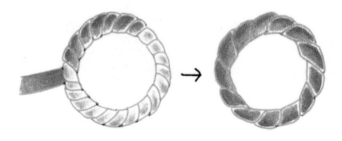

5. Wrap fabric E around quilt batting. Glue both ends of fabric to secure.

Make Decorations
[Red pepper]

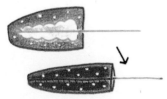

1. Cut a #26 stem wire into 1/4" and loop 5mm of one end. Wrap polyfil around the loop.

2. Cover the polyfil with red-pepper fabric and slipstich to secure.

3. Make a hole in the middle of the calyx fabric. Insert red-pepper wire through the hole, attach calyx fabric to red pepper and glue to secure. Arrange the shape of the red pepper.

[Holly berry]

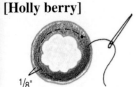

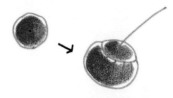

1. Stitch around the berry fabric, 1/8" inside of raw edges. Leave thread attached. Place polyfil in the center.

2. Pull thread to gather tightly. Cut a #26 stem wire into 4", place glue on one end, and insert it into the opening.

3. Make a hole in the center of back fabric of berry, insert berry wire through it and glue to secure.

[Leaf]

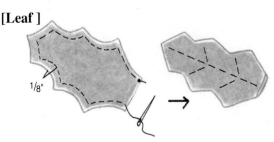

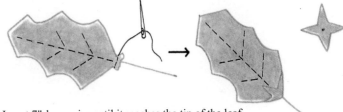

2. Insert 7"-long wire until it reaches the tip of the leaf. Gather the opening around the wire and stitch to secure. Make a hole in the center of calyx fabric, insert leaf wire through the hole, and glue to secure.

1. Layer 2 pieces of leaf fabric, right sides facing in, and stitch around 1/8" inside. Leave opening unstitched. Turn right side out. Stitch leaf veins with 2 strands of embroidery floss.

Assembly

Ribbon length: 20"

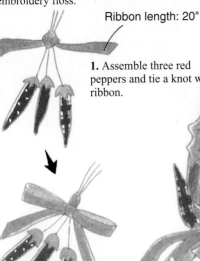

1. Assemble three red peppers and tie a knot with ribbon.

2. Tie into a bow and glue to wreath.

4. Make holes on both sides of berries with an awl and insert leaf wires with glue. Apply glue on the backside of leaves and attach them to wreath.

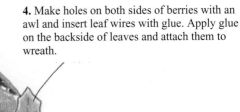

3. Twist together the wires of three berries and trim away, leaving 3/8" length. Make a hole into the wreath with an awl and insert berries into the wires and glue.

44/45   BOUQUET POMANDER AND GLOVES

A fabric bouquet pomander with a silk ribbon loop handle. Enhance originality with your choice of colors for roses and marguerites. Attach matching white marguerites on white lacy gloves.

44

45

Preparation: Referring to page 113, cut necessary numbers of fabric and other parts.

Materials for Bouquet Pomander:
Rose : 32" x 1 yd solid rose pink fabric
Marguerite : 22" x 14" solid white fabric
Center for Marguerite : 6" x 2" solid orange fabric
Small flowers : 28" x 8" solid pink fabric
Center for small flower : 8" x 2" solid yellow fabric
Leaves : 32" x 1 yd solid green fabric
12" x 2" quilt batting, 4" x 2" cardboard, 1" x 3 yds batting strip, 5 yds chunky wool yarn, 129 3mm pearl beads, 1½"-wide 1.3 yds ribbon, 1 4"-diam. styrofoam sphere, Setting pins, Craft glue, #1 (1/8") tube turner, #2 (3/16") tube turner

Materials for Gloves ornament:
Marguerite : 16" x 32" white fabric
Center for Marguerite : 6" x 2" solid orange fabric
Leaves : 12" x 6" green fabric
3" x 2" quilt batting, 2" x 2" cardboard, 1" x 1 yd batting strip, 30 3mm pearl beads, #2 (3/16") tube turner
★Sew onto lace gloves.

Make 13 Roses

Overlap.
3 small petals
1/4"
Overlap.

Overlap.
5 large petals
1/4"

4 large petals
1/4"

2. Pull thread of the 3 small petals to gather, and knot off.
Attach 3 pearl beads to the center.

1. Fold all rose petal fabrics in half. Take 3 small petal pieces and overlap each by 1/3 to form a circle. Gather stitch around edges, 1/4" inside. Repeat with 4 large petals and 5 large petals until 13 units of three types are made. Leave thread attached.

3. Place one 3 small petal unit into the 4 large petal unit, and pull thread to gather. Knot off.

small petal unit
Fold back.
Pull thread to gather.
Place inside.
Fold back 1/4" of each petal.
large 4-petal unit
Glue to secure petals.

Glue to secure petals.
Fold back 1/4" of each petal. Make 13.

4. Place the joined unit into a 5 large petals unit and pull thread to gather. Knot off.

Make Leaves
Make leaves and attach to their respective flowers.

leaf
Gather-stitch 1/4" inside the top edge.

Fold in half two times to make a triangle.

Pull thread to gather.

Sew onto the underside of flower.

Make 6 Large Marguerites

1. Refer to page 76 to make a fabric loop for the petals. Cut loop into 9 pieces.

Use #2 tube turner
18"
2"
petal fabric stuffed with batting strip.
Cut into 9 equal parts.

2. Fold each petal loop in half, and stitch along the lower edge of them to form a circle.

Fold to hide seam inside.
1/8"
Stitch 9 pieces together.

Form a circle and pull thread tightly

3. Make center of flower.

center of flower (back)
cardboard
quilt batting
1/8"
Pull thread.

center of flower

4. Place center of flower in the blossom, and stitch to secure. Glue on peal beads around the center. Attach leaf to back of petals. Make 6.

Glue 15 pearl beads
leaf
Slipstitch center.

Make 4 Small Marguerites

1. Refer to page 76 to make a fabric loop for the petals. Cut loop into 9 pieces. Work in the same manner as large marguerites to make 4 with pink fabric.

Use #1 tube turner.
7"
petal fabric stuffed with 2 pcs. yarn
3/4"
Cut into 9.

2. Gather stitch the base of 3 pieces of leaf to form a circle and pull thread to gather.

Pull thread to gather.

3. Glue 3 flowers onto the center of three leaves. Make 4.

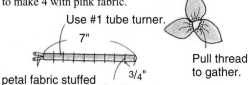
Glue.

Assembly
Glue ribbon to styrofoam as shown. Glue on the flowers in a balanced manner.
Attach ribbon bow at the base of the handle. Stitch marguerites to gloves.

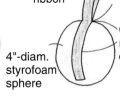
26"-long ribbon
7"
4"-diam. styrofoam sphere

Attach flowers to sphere with setting pins and glue.
Glue remaining ribbon on both sides.
13 roses

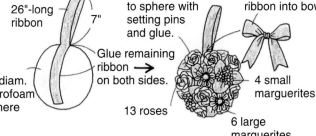
Tie 20"-long ribbon into bow.
4 small marguerites
6 large marguerites

Create corsages of your favorite flowers and decorate with ribbons.

Assemble 3 medium florets, 1 each of medium and small leaf, and tie with a satin ribbon.

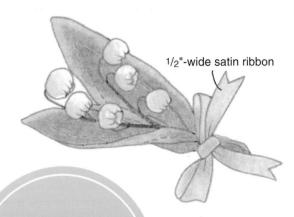

1/2"-wide satin ribbon

47   LILY OF THE VALLEY CORSAGE

Refreshing, pure white florets of lily of the valley make a delicate small corsage.
◆ Patterns on page 84
◆ Materials and instructions on page 29

46   POPPY CORSAGE

A combination of a blooming poppy and opening bud.
◆ Patterns on page 83
◆ Materials and instructions on page 26

1"-wide ribbon

Assemble one flower and one bud, fold the stems and tie with a ribbon.

2 1/4"

BASIC TECHNIQUES

How to use actual-size patterns:

book
tracing paper

Copy first the actual-size patterns. Place tracing paper on the relevant page and draw over the outlines. Always copy the fabric grains and openings.

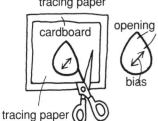

cardboard
tracing paper
opening
bias

Glue tracing paper onto cardboard and cut along the outlines. Circles and small squares that are not shown in actual size should be drawn directly on cardboard, then cut out.

General supplies and tools:

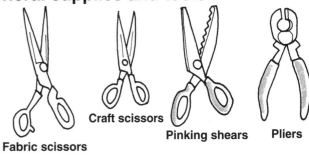

Craft scissors
Fabric scissors
Pinking shears
Pliers

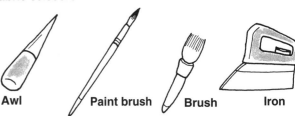

Awl
Paint brush
Brush
Iron

Apply glue to fabric:

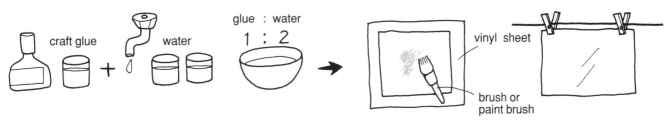

craft glue
water
glue : water
1 : 2
vinyl sheet
brush or paint brush

Use craft glue or fabric glue (water-soluble glue which becomes transparent when dried). Mix one part of glue into two parts of water.

Place fabric on a vinyl sheet and coat it with glue solution.

Smooth out creases and dry in the shade.

Mark fabric grain:

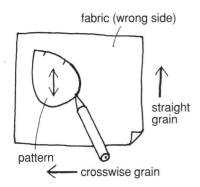

fabric (wrong side)
straight grain
pattern
crosswise grain

Place pattern on wrong side of fabric, matching the grain of the fabric marked on pattern. Trace the pattern onto fabric with an HB pencil or a tailor's chalk.

Cut fabric:

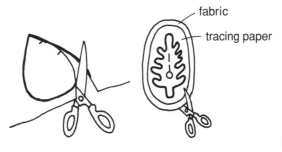

fabric
tracing paper

Cut out fabric inside of the traced outlines. For smaller items such as cosmos leaves, cut out fabric first into an appropriate size, secure tracing paper to fabric with dress pins so that fabric won't shift, then cut out along the pattern.

Attach adhesive interlining:

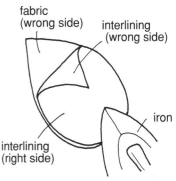

fabric (wrong side)
interlining (wrong side)
iron
interlining (right side)

Lay fabric and adhesive interlining wrong sides together, and press with iron to adhere.

Types of wires

● Stem wire

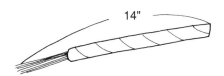

These are 14"-long and are sold in packs. There are plain, unwrapped types which are silver in color, and paper-wrapped types which are green or white. Gauge numbers vary according to its thickness, like #16, #20, and #30. The larger the number, the thinner the wire.

● Extra-thick stem wire

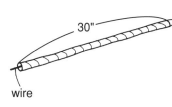

Specially made for flower stem, this sturdy wire is thickly covered with cardborad to save you from wrapping procedure. Sold in different sizes.

● Spool wire

This type wire is sold in turns of 12 ft.

How to wrap floral tape:

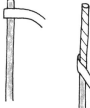

Place floral tape at right angle to wire and start wrapping. Lightly pull the tape as you turn the wire around, and wrap tape diagonally. Finish end by folding back the tape to cover bottom edge.

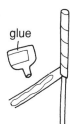

When using fabric tape instead of floral tape, apply a thin line of glue to the backside of it as you wrap down.

How to Use Tube Turner:

If tube turner is not available, use a "loop turner".

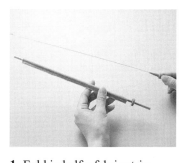

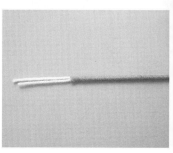

1. Fold in half a fabric strip, right sides facing in, and stitch lengthwise along the edge to make a fabric tube. Insert tube turner into fabric tube as straight as possible, making sure that stitches don't get twisted.

2. Insert wire hook to hook the crease at the end of fabric strip.

3. Hook wool yarn or strip batting strip to wire hook and pull wire. Once the tip of the hook has appeared, twist and remove hook. Pull loop from tube.

4. For #1 tube turner, fold in half a 3/4"-wide fabric strip, right side in, and stitch into 3/16" width. Insert 2 pieces of thick wool yarn. For #2 tube turner, fold in half a 1"-wide fabric strip, right side in, and stitch into 3/8" width. Insert a 1"-wide batting strip.

Embroidery Stitches

Back stitch	Straight stitch	Stem stitch

French knot stitch	Satin stitch

Lazy Daisy stitch (Chain stitch)	Overcast stitch

side of applique

ACTUAL-SIZE PATTERNS AND DRAWINGS

☆Seam allowance included

1 CHERRY BLOSSOMS on page 4

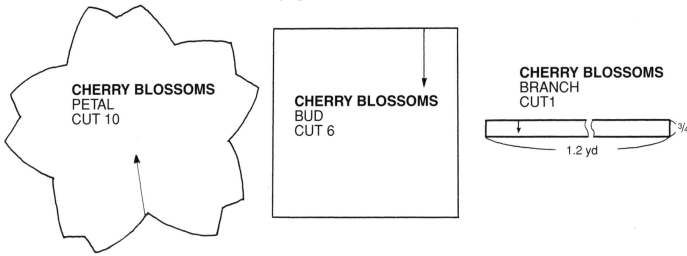

CHERRY BLOSSOMS
PETAL
CUT 10

CHERRY BLOSSOMS
BUD
CUT 6

CHERRY BLOSSOMS
BRANCH
CUT1

3/4"

1.2 yd

2 TULIP on page 6

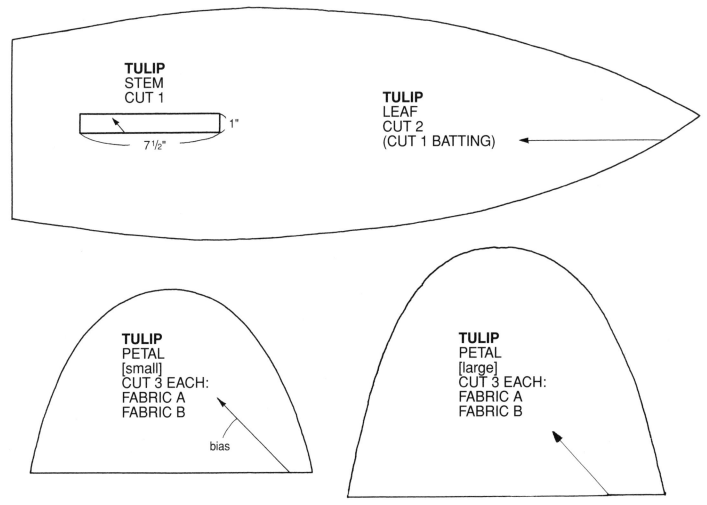

TULIP
STEM
CUT 1

1"

7½"

TULIP
LEAF
CUT 2
(CUT 1 BATTING)

TULIP
PETAL
[small]
CUT 3 EACH:
FABRIC A
FABRIC B

bias

TULIP
PETAL
[large]
CUT 3 EACH:
FABRIC A
FABRIC B

3 TULIP on page 8

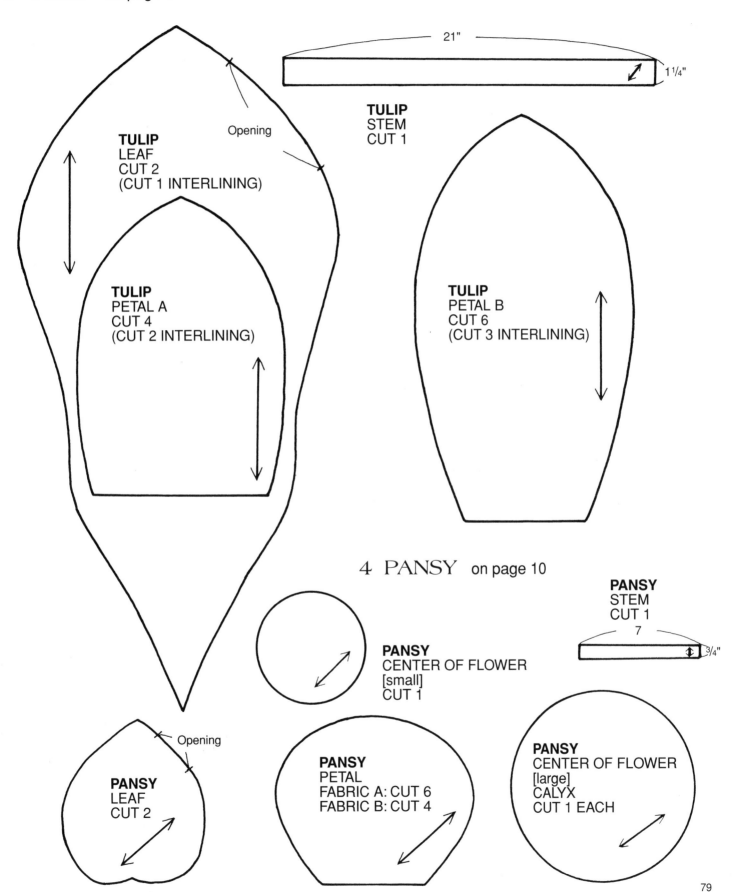

TULIP
LEAF
CUT 2
(CUT 1 INTERLINING)

Opening

TULIP
STEM
CUT 1

21"

1 1/4"

TULIP
PETAL A
CUT 4
(CUT 2 INTERLINING)

TULIP
PETAL B
CUT 6
(CUT 3 INTERLINING)

4 PANSY on page 10

PANSY
CENTER OF FLOWER
[small]
CUT 1

PANSY
STEM
CUT 1

7

3/4"

PANSY
LEAF
CUT 2

Opening

PANSY
PETAL
FABRIC A: CUT 6
FABRIC B: CUT 4

PANSY
CENTER OF FLOWER
[large]
CALYX
CUT 1 EACH

ACTUAL-SIZE PATTERNS AND DRAWINGS

☆ Seam allowance included

5 GARDEN STOCK   on page 12

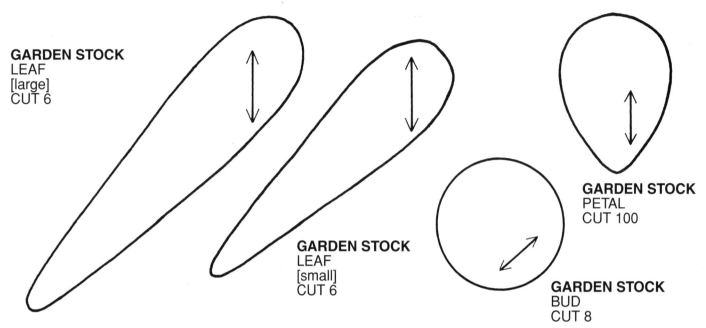

GARDEN STOCK
LEAF
[large]
CUT 6

GARDEN STOCK
LEAF
[small]
CUT 6

GARDEN STOCK
PETAL
CUT 100

GARDEN STOCK
BUD
CUT 8

6 SWEET PEA   on page 14

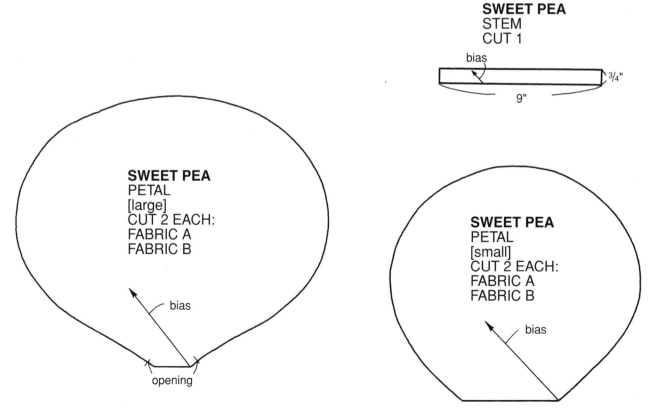

SWEET PEA
STEM
CUT 1

bias

3/4"

9"

SWEET PEA
PETAL
[large]
CUT 2 EACH:
FABRIC A
FABRIC B

bias

opening

SWEET PEA
PETAL
[small]
CUT 2 EACH:
FABRIC A
FABRIC B

bias

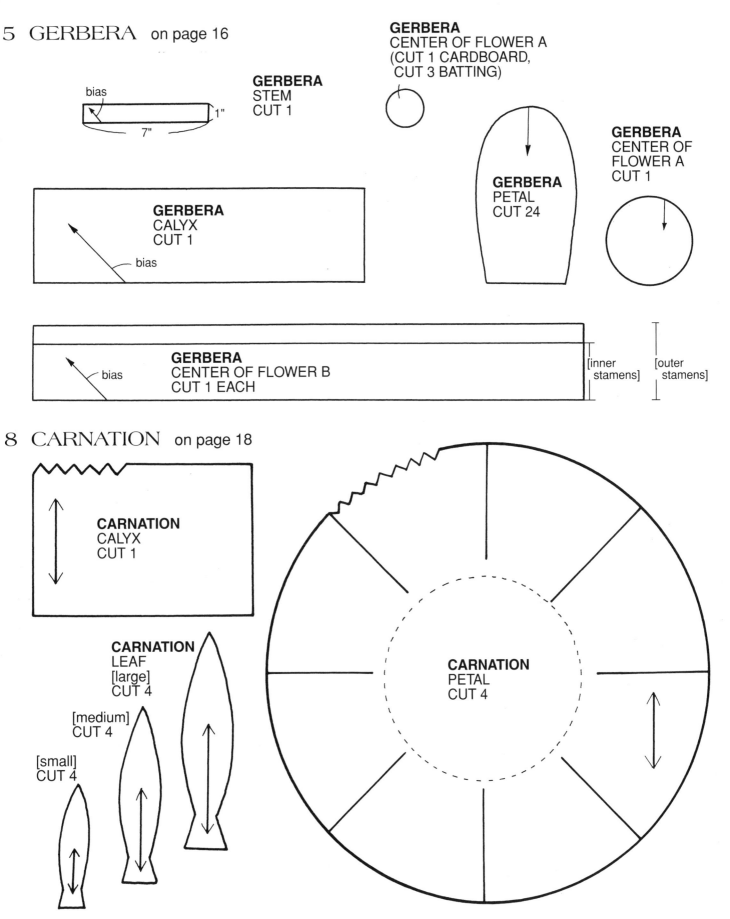

5 GERBERA on page 16

bias

1"

7"

GERBERA
STEM
CUT 1

GERBERA
CENTER OF FLOWER A
(CUT 1 CARDBOARD,
CUT 3 BATTING)

GERBERA
CALYX
CUT 1

bias

GERBERA
PETAL
CUT 24

GERBERA
CENTER OF
FLOWER A
CUT 1

GERBERA
CENTER OF FLOWER B
CUT 1 EACH

bias

[inner
stamens]

[outer
stamens]

8 CARNATION on page 18

CARNATION
CALYX
CUT 1

CARNATION
LEAF
[large]
CUT 4

[medium]
CUT 4

[small]
CUT 4

CARNATION
PETAL
CUT 4

ACTUAL-SIZE PATTERNS AND DRAWINGS

☆Seam allowance included

9 ROSE on page 20

ROSE
CALYX
CUT 1

ROSE
PETAL
[small]
CUT 2

ROSE
LEAF
[large]
CUT 2

ROSE
LEAF
[small]
CUT4

ROSE
PETAL
[large]
CUT 3

ROSE
STEM
CUT 1

24"

3/8"

10 ROSE on page 22

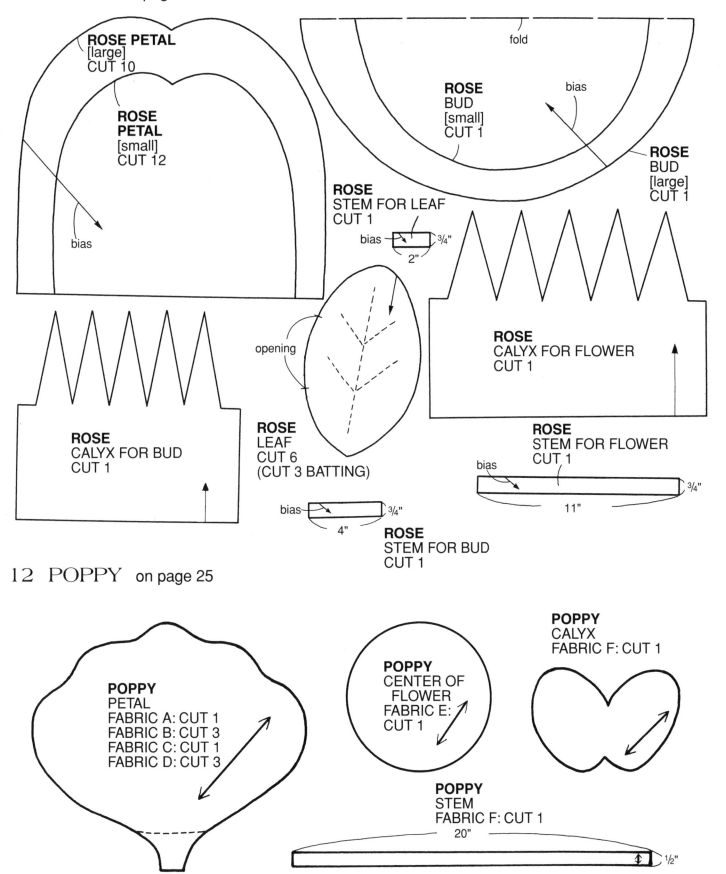

ROSE PETAL
[large]
CUT 10

ROSE PETAL
[small]
CUT 12

bias

fold

ROSE
BUD
[small]
CUT 1

bias

ROSE
BUD
[large]
CUT 1

ROSE
STEM FOR LEAF
CUT 1

bias

3/4"

2"

opening

ROSE
LEAF
CUT 6
(CUT 3 BATTING)

ROSE
CALYX FOR FLOWER
CUT 1

ROSE
CALYX FOR BUD
CUT 1

ROSE
STEM FOR FLOWER
CUT 1

bias

11"

3/4"

bias

4"

3/4"

ROSE
STEM FOR BUD
CUT 1

12 POPPY on page 25

POPPY
PETAL
FABRIC A: CUT 1
FABRIC B: CUT 3
FABRIC C: CUT 1
FABRIC D: CUT 3

POPPY
CENTER OF
FLOWER
FABRIC E:
CUT 1

POPPY
CALYX
FABRIC F: CUT 1

POPPY
STEM
FABRIC F: CUT 1

20"

1/2"

13 LILY OF THE VALLEY on page 28

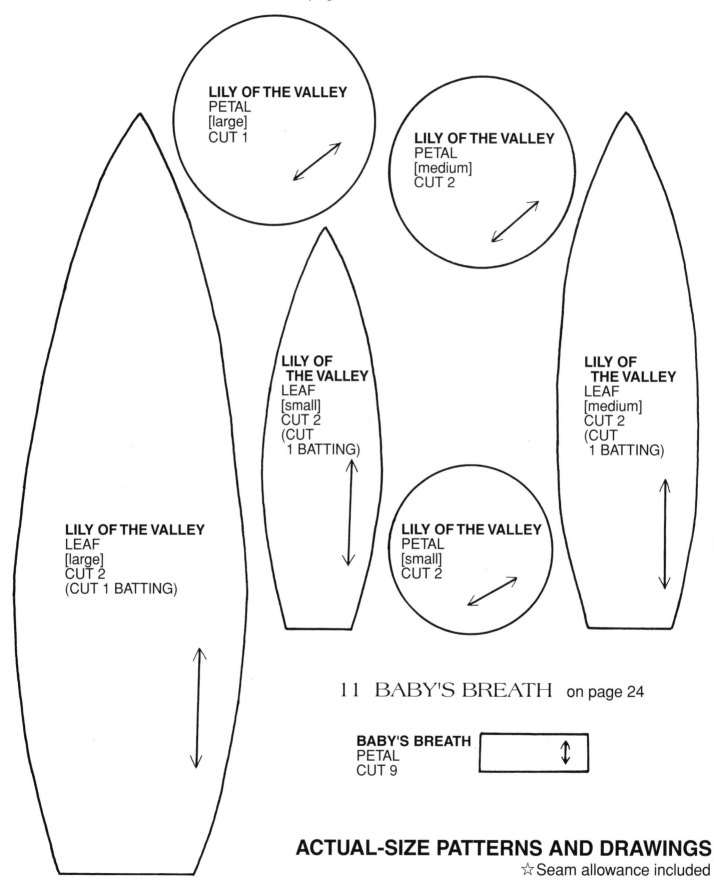

LILY OF THE VALLEY
PETAL
[large]
CUT 1

LILY OF THE VALLEY
PETAL
[medium]
CUT 2

LILY OF THE VALLEY
LEAF
[small]
CUT 2
(CUT
 1 BATTING)

LILY OF THE VALLEY
LEAF
[large]
CUT 2
(CUT 1 BATTING)

LILY OF THE VALLEY
PETAL
[small]
CUT 2

**LILY OF
 THE VALLEY**
LEAF
[medium]
CUT 2
(CUT
 1 BATTING)

11 BABY'S BREATH on page 24

BABY'S BREATH
PETAL
CUT 9

ACTUAL-SIZE PATTERNS AND DRAWINGS
☆Seam allowance included

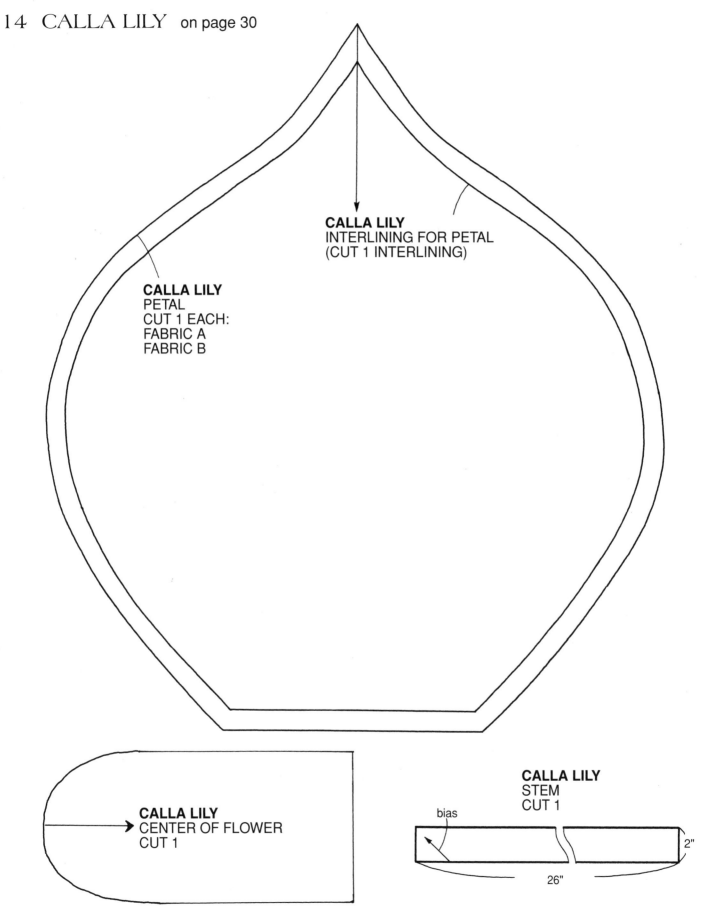

CALLA LILY
INTERLINING FOR PETAL
(CUT 1 INTERLINING)

CALLA LILY
PETAL
CUT 1 EACH:
FABRIC A
FABRIC B

CALLA LILY
CENTER OF FLOWER
CUT 1

CALLA LILY
STEM
CUT 1

bias

2"

26"

ACTUAL-SIZE PATTERNS AND DRAWINGS

☆ Seam allowance included

15 CALLA LILY on page 32

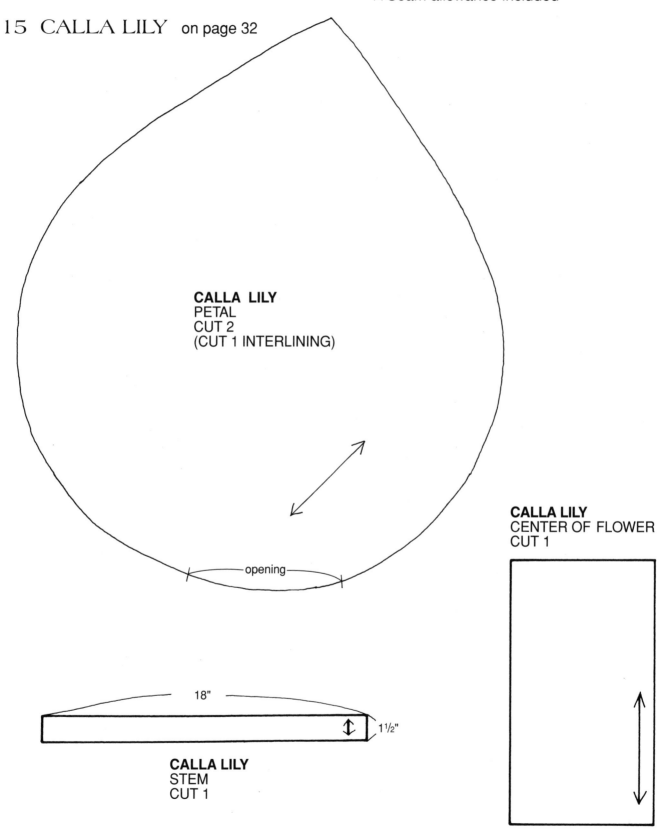

CALLA LILY
PETAL
CUT 2
(CUT 1 INTERLINING)

opening

CALLA LILY
CENTER OF FLOWER
CUT 1

18"

1½"

CALLA LILY
STEM
CUT 1

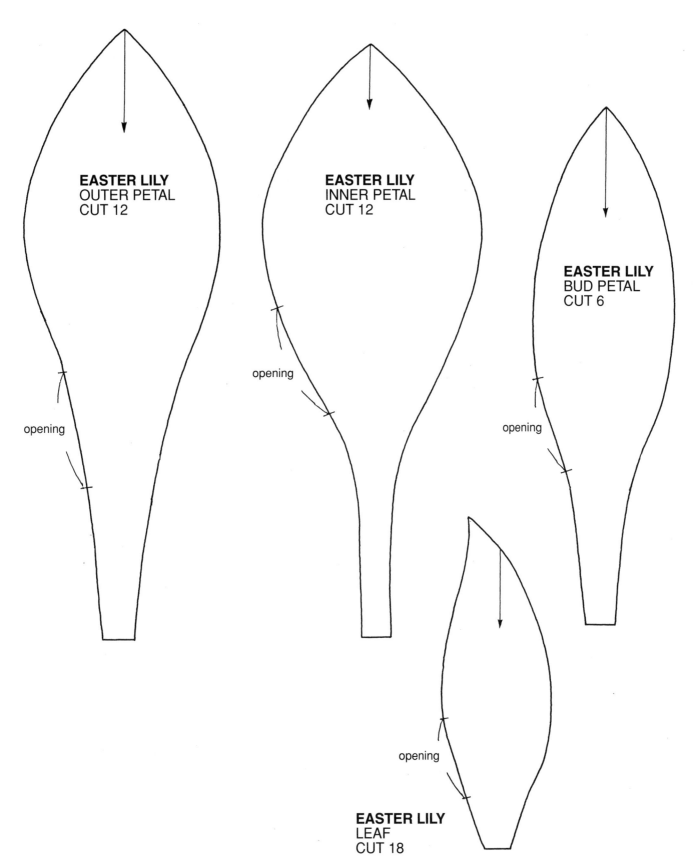

EASTER LILY
OUTER PETAL
CUT 12

opening

EASTER LILY
INNER PETAL
CUT 12

opening

EASTER LILY
BUD PETAL
CUT 6

opening

EASTER LILY
LEAF
CUT 18

opening

17 HYDRANGEA on page 36

ACTUAL-SIZE PATTERNS AND DRAWINGS

☆Seam allowance included

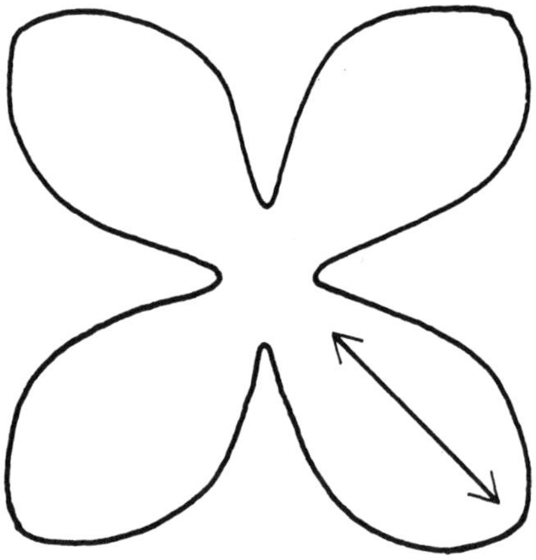

HYDRANGEA
PETAL
FABRIC A: CUT 8
FABRIC B: CUT 4
FABRIC C: CUT 3
FABRIC D: CUT 6

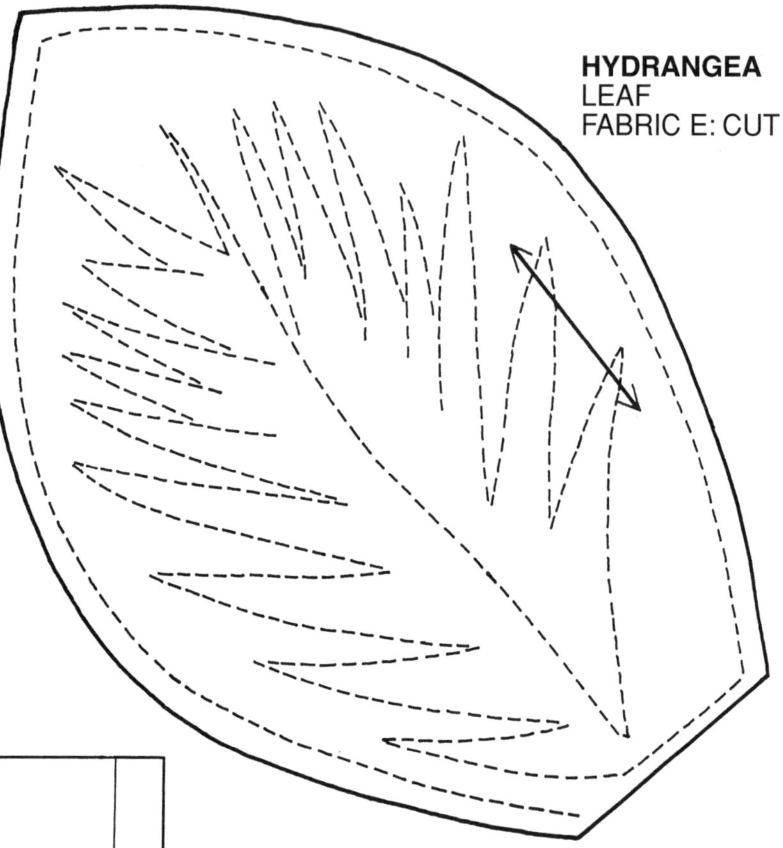

HYDRANGEA
LEAF
FABRIC E: CUT 2

20 CLEMATIS on page 42

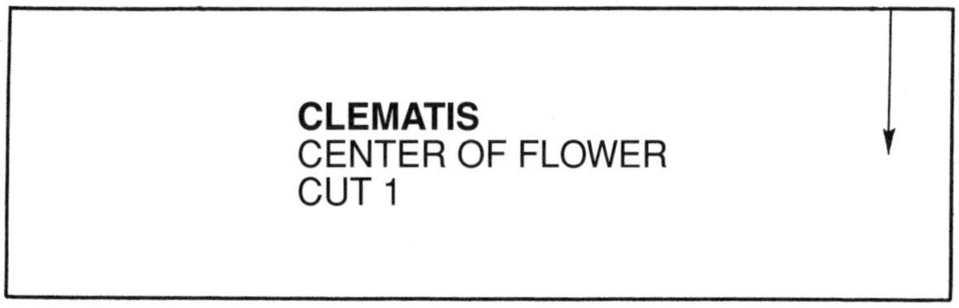
CLEMATIS
CENTER OF FLOWER
CUT 1

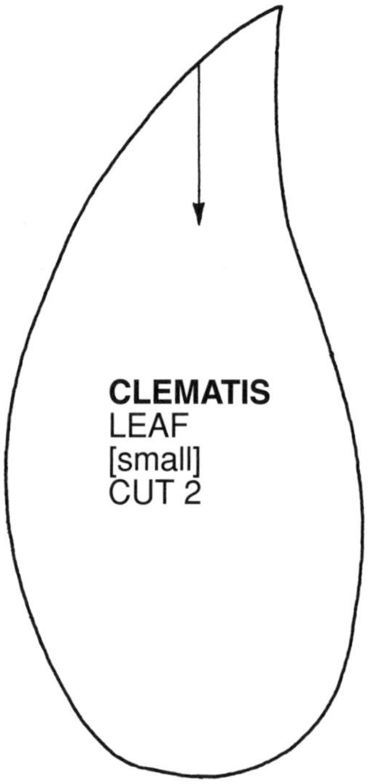
CLEMATIS
LEAF
[small]
CUT 2

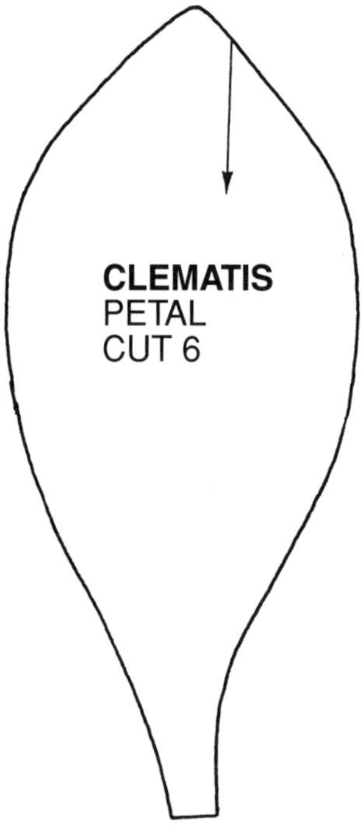
CLEMATIS
PETAL
CUT 6

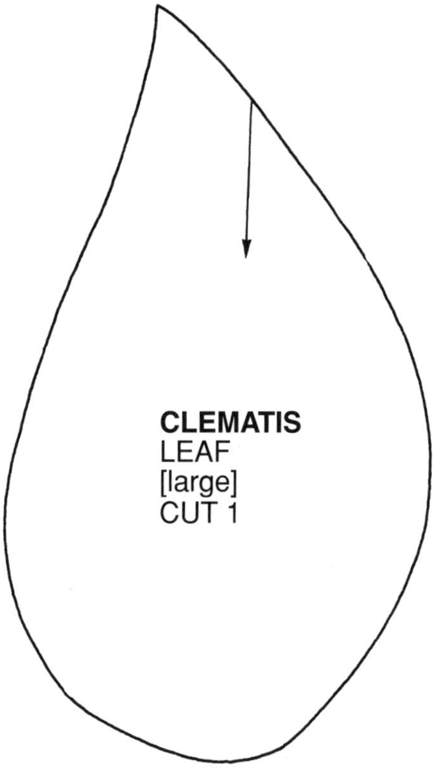
CLEMATIS
LEAF
[large]
CUT 1

18 SUNFLOWER on page 38

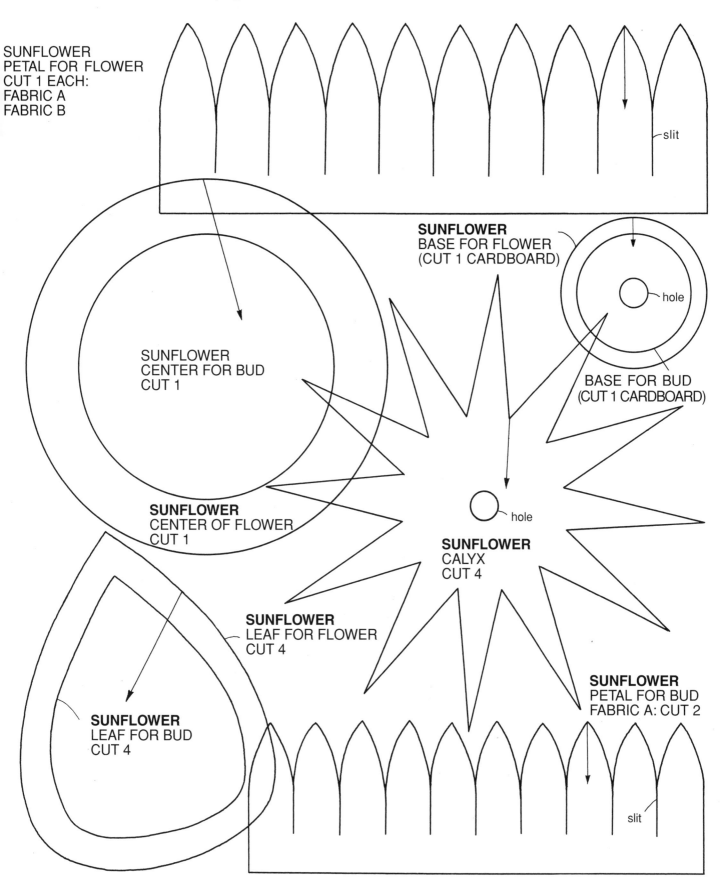

SUNFLOWER
PETAL FOR FLOWER
CUT 1 EACH:
FABRIC A
FABRIC B

slit

SUNFLOWER
BASE FOR FLOWER
(CUT 1 CARDBOARD)

hole

SUNFLOWER
CENTER FOR BUD
CUT 1

BASE FOR BUD
(CUT 1 CARDBOARD)

SUNFLOWER
CENTER OF FLOWER
CUT 1

hole

SUNFLOWER
CALYX
CUT 4

SUNFLOWER
LEAF FOR FLOWER
CUT 4

SUNFLOWER
PETAL FOR BUD
FABRIC A: CUT 2

SUNFLOWER
LEAF FOR BUD
CUT 4

slit

ACTUAL-SIZE PATTERNS AND DRAWINGS

☆Seam allowance included

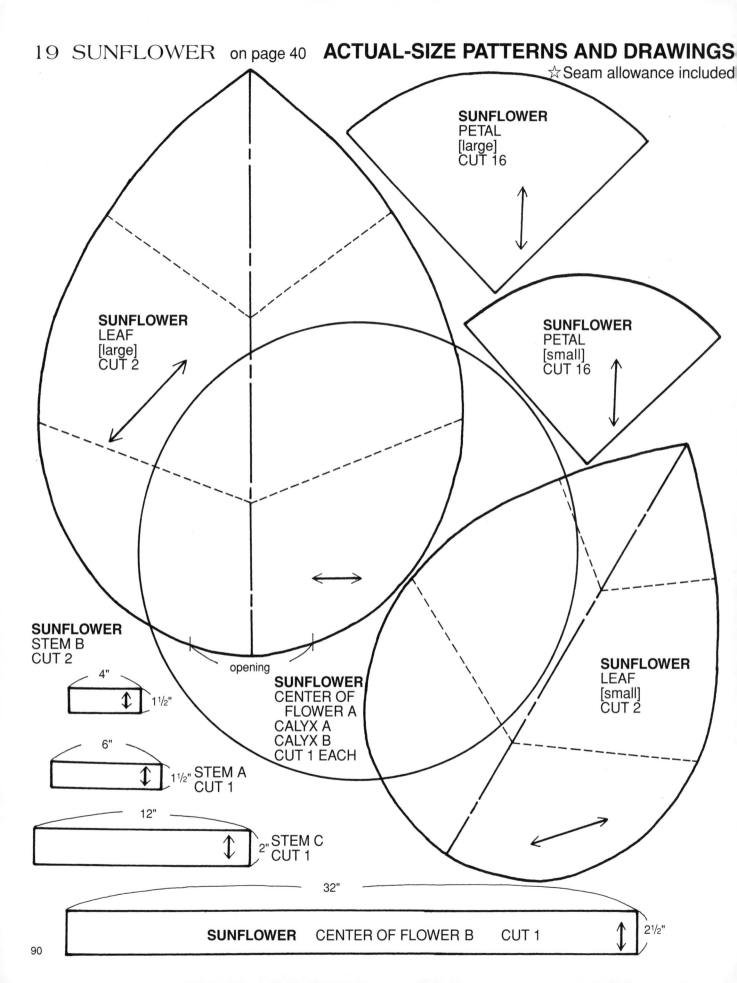

SUNFLOWER
PETAL
[large]
CUT 16

SUNFLOWER
LEAF
[large]
CUT 2

SUNFLOWER
PETAL
[small]
CUT 16

SUNFLOWER
STEM B
CUT 2

4"

1½"

SUNFLOWER
CENTER OF
FLOWER A
CALYX A
CALYX B
CUT 1 EACH

opening

SUNFLOWER
LEAF
[small]
CUT 2

6"

1½" STEM A
CUT 1

12"

2" STEM C
CUT 1

32"

SUNFLOWER   CENTER OF FLOWER B   CUT 1

2½"

21 GLORY LILY on page on page 44

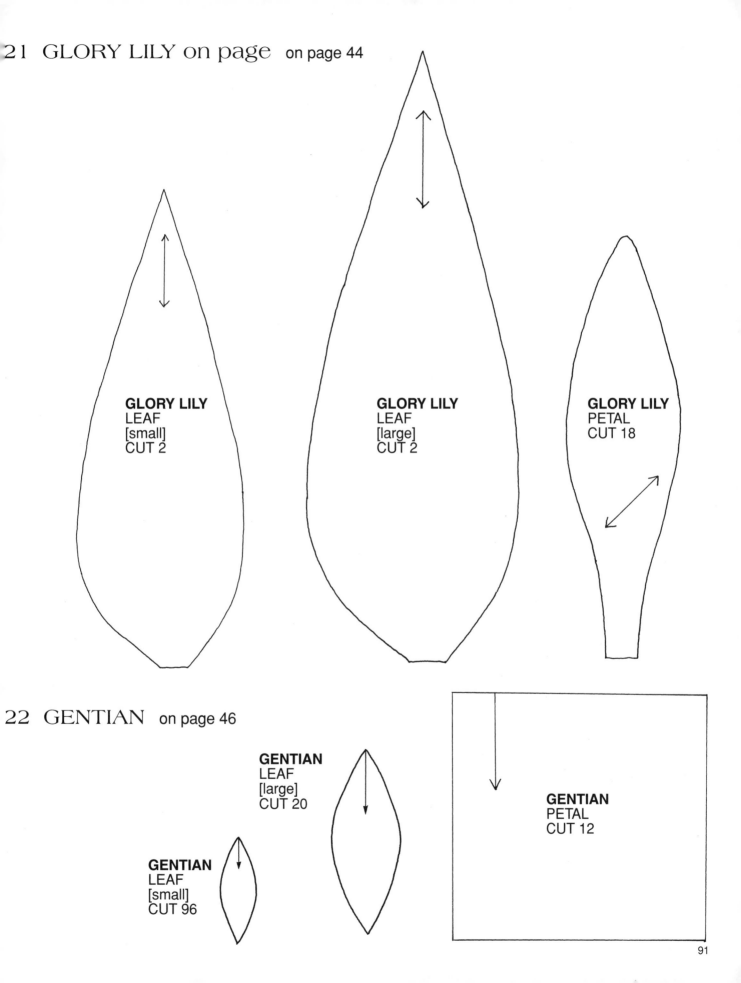

GLORY LILY
LEAF
[small]
CUT 2

GLORY LILY
LEAF
[large]
CUT 2

GLORY LILY
PETAL
CUT 18

22 GENTIAN on page 46

GENTIAN
LEAF
[large]
CUT 20

GENTIAN
LEAF
[small]
CUT 96

GENTIAN
PETAL
CUT 12

ACTUAL-SIZE PATTERNS AND DRAWINGS

☆Seam allowance included

23 CHINESE BELLFLOWER
on page 48

CHINESE BELLFLOWER
PETAL FOR LARGE BUD
CUT 1

CHINESE BELLFLOWER
CENTER OF FLOWER
[large]
CUT 2: FABRIC A

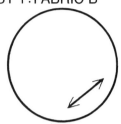

CHINESE BELLFLOWER
CENTER OF FLOWER
[small]
CUT 1: FABRIC B

CHINESE BELLFLOWER
PETAL FOR FLOWER
CUT 1

CHINESE BELLFLOWER
LEAF
[large]
CUT 4

LEAF
[small]
CUT 2

CHINESE BELLFLOWER
CALYX FOR SMALL BUD
CUT 1

CHINESE BELLFLOWER
CALYX FOR FLOWER
CUT 1

CHINESE BELLFLOWER
CALYX FOR LARGE BUD
CUT 1

CHINESE BELLFLOWER
STEM
CUT 1

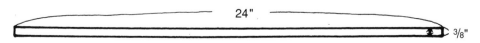

24"

3/8"

92

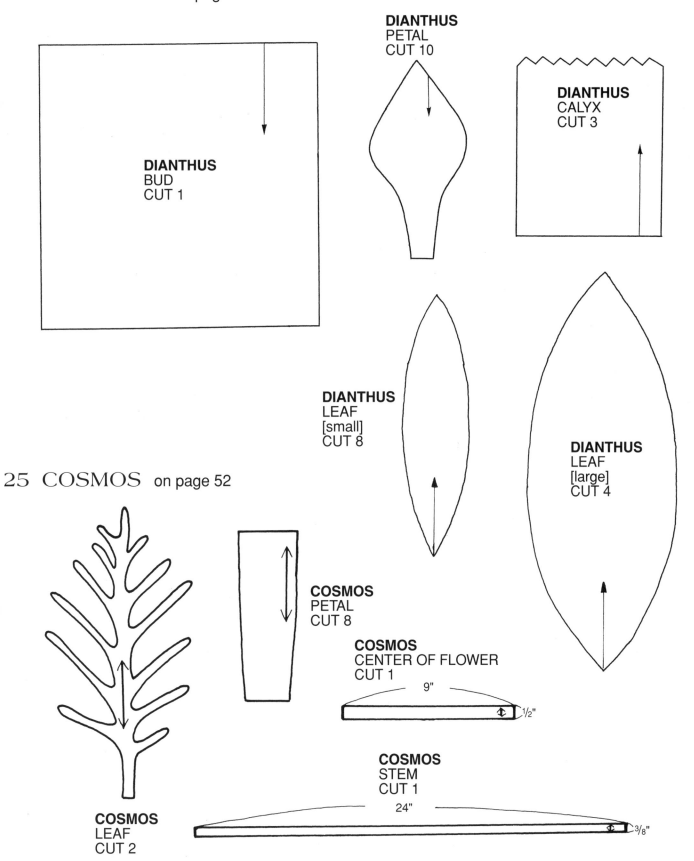

DIANTHUS
PETAL
CUT 10

DIANTHUS
CALYX
CUT 3

DIANTHUS
BUD
CUT 1

DIANTHUS
LEAF
[small]
CUT 8

DIANTHUS
LEAF
[large]
CUT 4

25 COSMOS on page 52

COSMOS
PETAL
CUT 8

COSMOS
CENTER OF FLOWER
CUT 1

9"

1/2"

COSMOS
STEM
CUT 1

24"

3/8"

COSMOS
LEAF
CUT 2

ACTUAL-SIZE PATTERNS AND DRAWINGS
☆Seam allowance included

29 GOLDEN MIMOSA on page 58

MIMOSA
LEAF
CUT 18

26 GREAT BURNET on page 54

GREAT BURNET
LEAF
CUT 4

GREAT BURNET
PETAL
CUT 4: FABRIC A
CUT 2: FABRIC B
CUT 1: FABRIC C

28 CORNFLOWER on page 56

slit

CORNFLOWER
CALYX FOR BUD
CUT 1

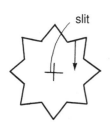

CORNFLOWER
BUD
CUT 1

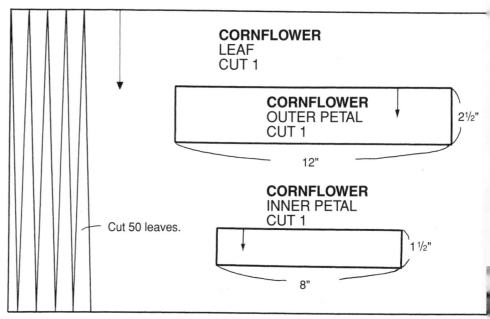

Cut 50 leaves.

CORNFLOWER
LEAF
CUT 1

CORNFLOWER
OUTER PETAL
CUT 1

2½"

12"

CORNFLOWER
INNER PETAL
CUT 1

1½"

8"

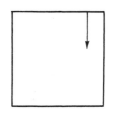

CORNFLOWER
CALYX FOR FLOWER
CUT 1

27 ALLIUM GIGANTEUM
on page 55

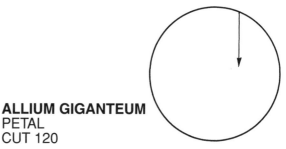

ALLIUM GIGANTEUM
PETAL
CUT 120

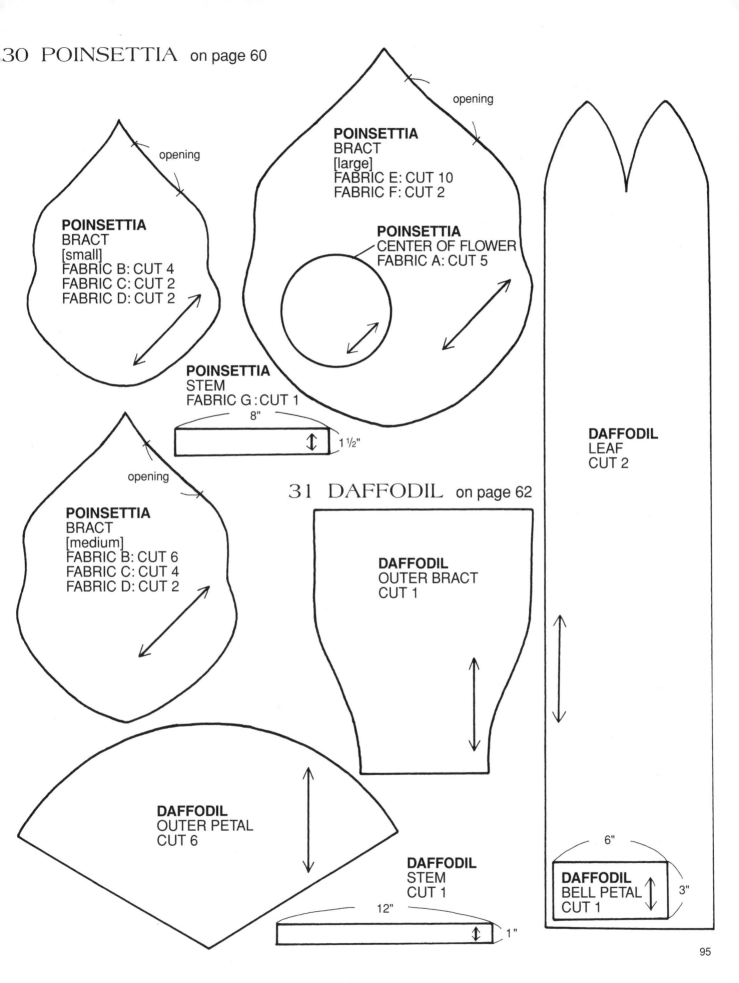

30 POINSETTIA on page 60

POINSETTIA
BRACT
[small]
FABRIC B: CUT 4
FABRIC C: CUT 2
FABRIC D: CUT 2

opening

POINSETTIA
BRACT
[large]
FABRIC E: CUT 10
FABRIC F: CUT 2

opening

POINSETTIA
CENTER OF FLOWER
FABRIC A: CUT 5

POINSETTIA
STEM
FABRIC G : CUT 1

8"

1 1/2"

DAFFODIL
LEAF
CUT 2

31 DAFFODIL on page 62

POINSETTIA
BRACT
[medium]
FABRIC B: CUT 6
FABRIC C: CUT 4
FABRIC D: CUT 2

opening

DAFFODIL
OUTER BRACT
CUT 1

DAFFODIL
OUTER PETAL
CUT 6

DAFFODIL
STEM
CUT 1

12"

1"

6"

DAFFODIL
BELL PETAL
CUT 1

3"

32 FRAMED TULIPS on page 64

Materials

Petals: 4" x 8" purple fabric, 8" x 4" pink fabric, Leaves: 16" x 24" green fabric, Drapes/Tie-backs/Valance: 16" x 6" striped cotton, Background: 18" x 16" printed cotton, Scraps for applique, 5" ½"-wide cotton lace tape,

16" x 13" quilt batting,12 14"-long #26 wire, Craft glue, Polyfil, 16" x 13" styrofoam board, 16" x 13" cardboard, Thin plastic tube for stems, Embroidery floss, 16" x13" picture frame (inner measurments)

ACTUAL-SIZE PATTERNS AND DRAWINGS

☆Seam allowance included except applique parts

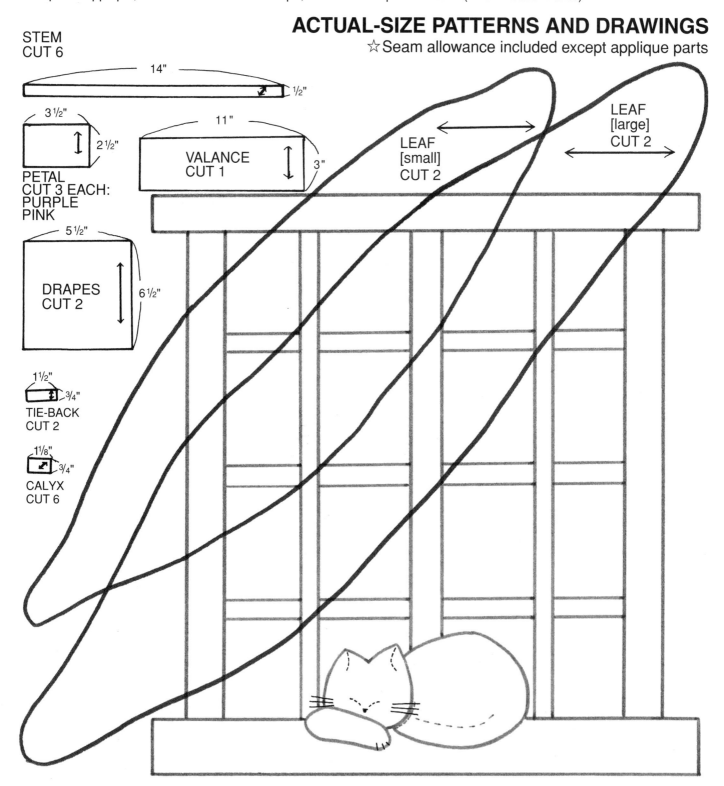

STEM
CUT 6

14"

½"

3½"

2½"

PETAL
CUT 3 EACH:
PURPLE
PINK

11"

VALANCE
CUT 1

3"

5½"

DRAPES
CUT 2

6½"

1½"

¾"

TIE-BACK
CUT 2

1⅛"

¾"

CALYX
CUT 6

LEAF
[small]
CUT 2

LEAF
[large]
CUT 2

96

Make Background

1. Applique window and cat to the ground fabric.

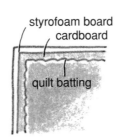

styrofoam board
cardboard
quilt batting

2. Layer styrofoam board, cardboard and quilt batting, then top with ground fabric.

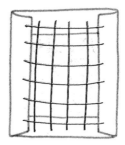

3. Turn back edges of the fabric, and secure all ends with sewing thread.

Make Flowers

1. To make stems, insert 2 wires into each plastic tube. Wrap with stem fabric and secure with glue.

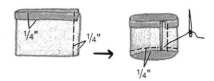

¼"　¼"　¼"

2. Turn back ¼" of petal fabric, and fold in half right sides facing in. Stitch side and lower edges.

3. Bend ¼" tip of wrapped stem, and wrap it with polyfil to make 1" sphere. Insert petal upside down, and pull thread to gather. Turn back petal.

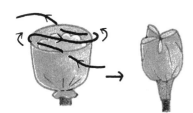

4. Divide circumference into quarters, and sew the four points as shown. Pull thread to gather at center. Knot off. Wrap the base with calyx fabric, and glue.

Make Leaves

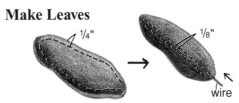

¼"　⅛"　wire

Layer 2 leaf parts right sides facing in, and stitch ¼" inside, leaving opening unstitched. Turn inside out. Stitch double center lines. Cut wire into 9" and 7", and insert each between stitches.

Make Valance

11"
opening
fold
1½"　¼"　5"　1"

Fold the fabric in half lengthwise (right sides facing in), and machine-stitch edges leaving the opening. Turn inside out and slipstitch to close opening. Gather-stitch to make ruffles.

Make Drapes

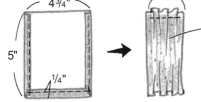

4¾"　1½"
5"　¼"

Turn back 3 edges and machine-stitch to secure. Stitch raw edge, gathering as you work. Make 2 and glue onto window pane.

Assembly

Secure by stitching stems onto ground fabric. Secure leaves hiding stitches.

5" lace

Machine-stitch lace tape over the valance, and stitch onto drapes.

Make Tie-backs

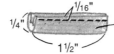

¼"　¹⁄₁₆"　1½"

Make tubes and "bind" the drapes with glue.

97

33 FRAMED HYDRANGEAS on page 65

Materials

Petals: 4" x 1 yd purple/lavender fabric, 26" x 4" blue fabric, 22" x 4" gray fabric, Leaves: 20" x 12" green fabric, 16" x12" olive green fabric, Background: 18" x16" printed fabric, Scraps for applique, 16" x 13" quilt batting, 22 14"-long #26 green wires, 8 large clear beads, 15 stamens, Craft glue, 16" x 13" 1/4"-thick styrofoam board, 16" x 13" cardboard, Embroidery floss, Green floral tape, 16" x 13" picture frame (inner measurements)

ACTUAL-SIZE PATTERNS AND DRAWINGS

☆Seam allowance included

●This applique pattern excludes seam allowance. Add about 1/8" allowance to cut out.

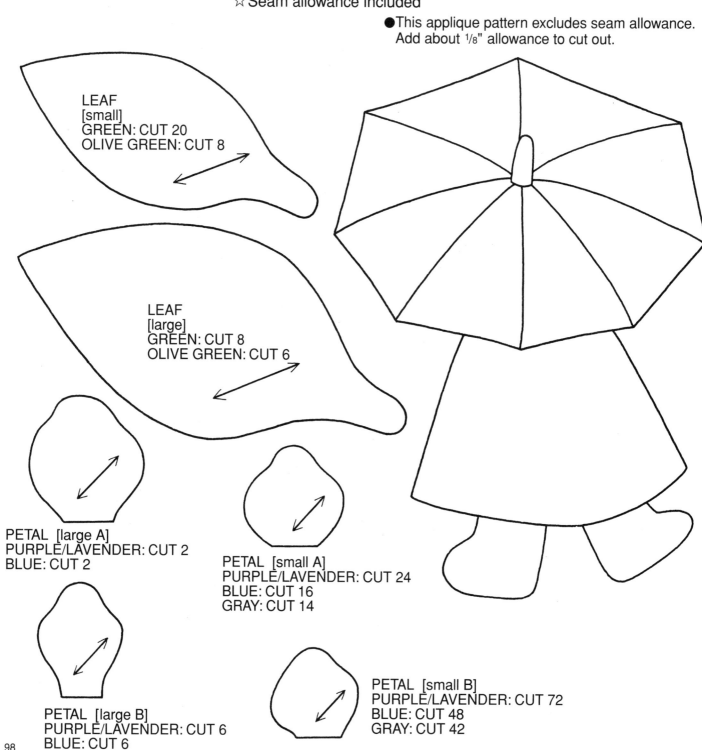

LEAF
[small]
GREEN: CUT 20
OLIVE GREEN: CUT 8

LEAF
[large]
GREEN: CUT 8
OLIVE GREEN: CUT 6

PETAL [large A]
PURPLE/LAVENDER: CUT 2
BLUE: CUT 2

PETAL [small A]
PURPLE/LAVENDER: CUT 24
BLUE: CUT 16
GRAY: CUT 14

PETAL [large B]
PURPLE/LAVENDER: CUT 6
BLUE: CUT 6

PETAL [small B]
PURPLE/LAVENDER: CUT 72
BLUE: CUT 48
GRAY: CUT 42

Make Background

1. Applique the girl with umbrella slightly below the center.

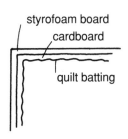

2. Layer styrofoam board, cardboard, then quilt batting.

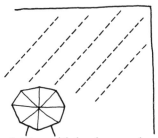

3. Top with background fabric matching at centers. Work straight stitch to embroider rain pattern.

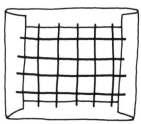

4. Turn back edges of the fabric and secure all ends with sewing thread.

Make Flowers

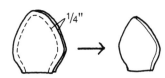

1. Layer 2 petal fabric parts right sides facing in, and stitch 1/4" inside, leaving opening unstitched. Turn right side out.

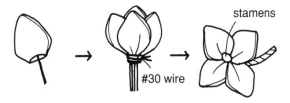

2. Insert 2" of #26 wire into the opening of the petal, and glue to secure. Cut stamens into halves, and add to the petal. Assemble 1 petal A and 3 petals B and bind with 2"-long #30 wire. Wrap with floral tape. Make 2 large, 27 small florets.

3. Coil the wrapped wire for a more three dimensional effect.

Make Leaves

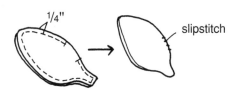

1. Layer 2 leaf fabric parts right sides facing in. Stitch 1/4" inside leaving opening unstitched. Turn right side out, and slipstitch to close the opening. Make 7 large, 14 small leaves.

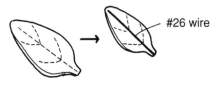

2. Machine-stitch veins as shown. Cut wire into 4" and 3" and glue onto backside of each large and small leaf.

Assembly

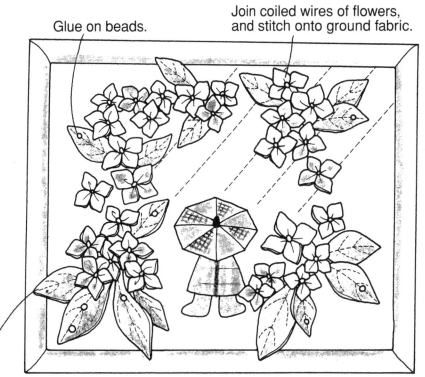

Glue on beads.

Join coiled wires of flowers, and stitch onto ground fabric.

Glue on leaves.

34 WILD ROSE BASKET on page 66

Materials
Petals:4" x 1 yd pink fabric, Center of flower: 2" x 1 yd yellow fabric, Leaves/Calyxes: 4" x 1 yd green fabric, Basket: 32" x 1 yd brown fabric, 12" x 1 yd checked pattern fabric, Backing: 12" x 8" brown fabric, Lining: 22" x 12" brown fabric,16" 2"-wide red check ribbon,

Appliqued mouse and cat: 8" square black felt, 2" square gray felt, Small pieces of white felt, red cotton, red check fabric, Background: 20" x 20" quilted fabric, 20" x 20" lining, 28"x1 yd quilt batting, Embroidery floss (black, blue, beige, light blue), Green floral tape, 17" x 14" cardboard, 82 #30 stem wires, Craft glue , 17"x 14" picture frame (inner measurements)

Preparation: Stiffen fabric for flowers and leaves by applying spray laundry starch several times.

Make Center of Flower

Make 1/8"-deep slits evenly spaced at 1/12".

center of flower 1/8"

Fold wire in half, and hook the fold on the nearest end slit of fabric.

Apply glue on fabric and tightly wrap around wire.

Glue stamens around center of flower.

Make Leaves

back

Cut wire into 7" and glue to the back of leaf.

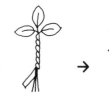

Join 3 leaves and secure with floral tape for 3-leaf unit. Make 20.

Make 5-leaf unit in the same manner. Make 14.

Make Flowers

petal

Dampen petal parts. Pressing and stretching with fingers, form a round depression in the middle of petals. Spray with laundry starch to stiffen.

Glue petals to center of flower.

Glue.

Make a hole in the center of 2 petals with an awl. Insert wire of center of flower through it.

Wrap stem with floral tape and attach 3-leaf unit. Be sure to attach a 3-leaf unit.

Glue calyx to flower base.

Make Borders of Basket

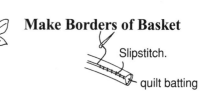

Slipstitch.

quilt batting

quilt batting

cardboard

lining

Weave Basket

Make:11 strips brown solid color
11 strips checked pattern

5/8"

Fold long edges toward center to make a tape.

Weave basket tapes on backing fabric.

Mark the shape of basket on woven tapes. Attach backing fabric to the woven tape, right sides facing in, by machine-stitching 1/12" outside the marking. Cut out basket.

backing

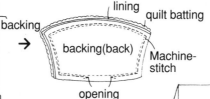

lining quilt batting

backing(back)

Machine-stitch

opening

Layer basket fabric and lining fabric, right sides facing in, then layer them on quilt batting, and stitch the three together. Leave opening unstitched. Turn basket right side out.

Make Basket Handle

1/8" handle(back)
1/8"

quilt batting Fold one side.

↓

Overlap and slipstitch.

3/8"

Front

Make 4 Types of Clusters:
A:8 flowers w/ six 5-leaf units: attach to 8½"-long wire
B:4 flowers w/ two 5-leaf units: attach to 4"-long wire
C:4 flowers w/ four 5-leaf units: attach to 12"-long wire
D:two 5-leaf units w/ four 3-leaf units: attach to 12"-long wire

●Add 1½" seam allowance all around ground fabric before cutting, and refer to page 104 for preparation.
●Attach flower stems by stitching several points onto ground fabric.

Twist together the two handle ropes and stitch onto ground fabric.

Attach **A** along the handle.

Assembly

(ground fabric)

Tie a bow.

C **B** **A**

17"

D

Slip-stitch.

Twist ends of wire.

Slipstitch.
Glue 3 leaves.

14"

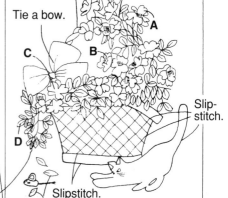

ACTUAL-SIZE PATTERNS AND DRAWINGS

☆Use 2-ply embroidery floss.

☆The numbers encircled represent the seam allowance. Cut out each part adding the allowance.

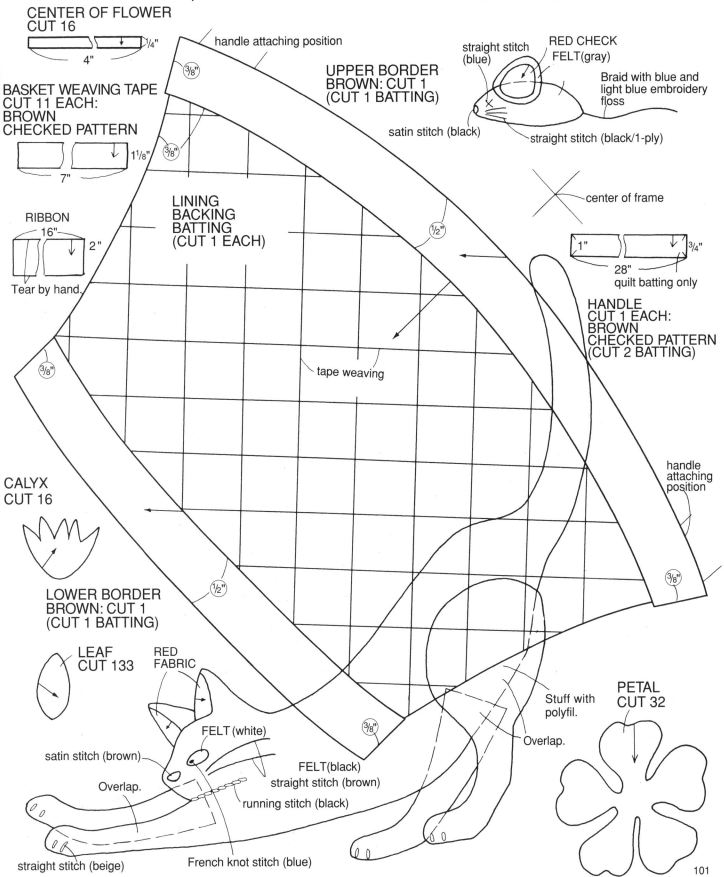

CENTER OF FLOWER CUT 16 — 4", 1/4"

BASKET WEAVING TAPE CUT 11 EACH: BROWN CHECKED PATTERN — 7", 1 1/8"

RIBBON — 16", 2", Tear by hand.

CALYX CUT 16

LEAF CUT 133

handle attaching position

UPPER BORDER BROWN: CUT 1 (CUT 1 BATTING)

LINING BACKING BATTING (CUT 1 EACH)

tape weaving

LOWER BORDER BROWN: CUT 1 (CUT 1 BATTING)

RED FABRIC

FELT (white)

satin stitch (brown)

Overlap.

straight stitch (beige)

French knot stitch (blue)

FELT (black)
straight stitch (brown)
running stitch (black)

straight stitch (blue)

RED CHECK FELT (gray)

satin stitch (black)

Braid with blue and light blue embroidery floss

straight stitch (black/1-ply)

center of frame

1", 3/4"
28"
quilt batting only

HANDLE CUT 1 EACH: BROWN CHECKED PATTERN (CUT 2 BATTING)

handle attaching position

Stuff with polyfil.

Overlap.

PETAL CUT 32

101

35 AUTUMN FLOWERS AT A MOONLIGHT PARTY on page 66

Materials

Petals: 16" x 2" random-dyed purple fabric, Centers of flower: 31" x 2" yellow fabric, Leaves/Calyxes: 20" x 8" random-dyed green fabric, Silver grass leaves: 8" x8" olive green print, Spikes of silver grass: 20" x 12" random-dyed brown fabric, Moon: 22" x 22" yellow print, Background: 19"x 17" navy print, Applique: 8" x 8" white felt, 3 #20 stem wires, 13 #28 stem wires, 12 #30 stem wires, 2 1/2"-diam. pompons, Green floral tape, 14" x 18" backing fabric, 32" x 42" quilt batting, Craft glue, 17" x 13" cardboard, 17" x 14" picture frame (inner measurements)

Preparation: Stiffen fabric for flowers and leaves by applying spray laundry starch several times.

Make Flowers

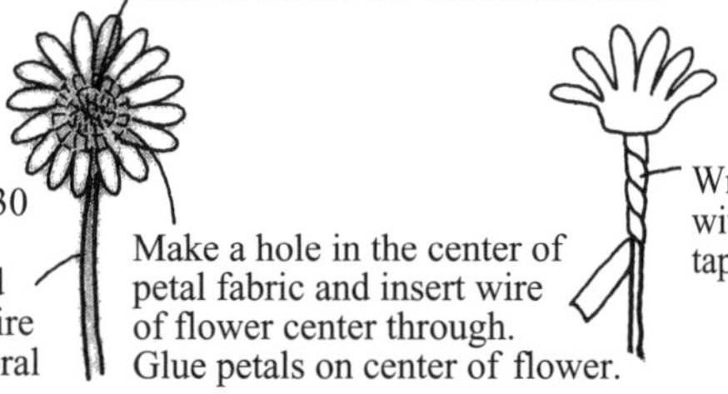

Refer to #34 to make center of flower but do not attach stamens.
Bend #30 wire in half and wrap wire with floral tape.
Make a hole in the center of petal fabric and insert wire of flower center through. Glue petals on center of flower.
Wrap wire with floral tape.

Make Leaves

Sandwich a 4" piece of #30 wire between 2 pieces of leaf fabric and glue together. Transfer leaf outline onto the fabric and then cut out leaf.

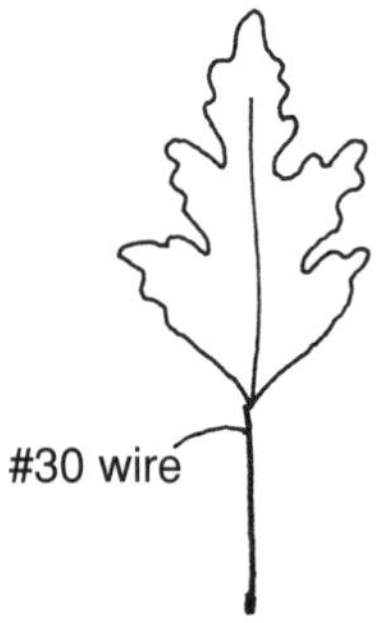

#30 wire

- Refer to page 104 to make the base of frame.
- Attach flowers and silver grass on ground fabric randomly as desired.
- Cut out ground fabric adding 1 1/2" seam allowance all around.
- Cut out moon adding 1/4" seam allowance.

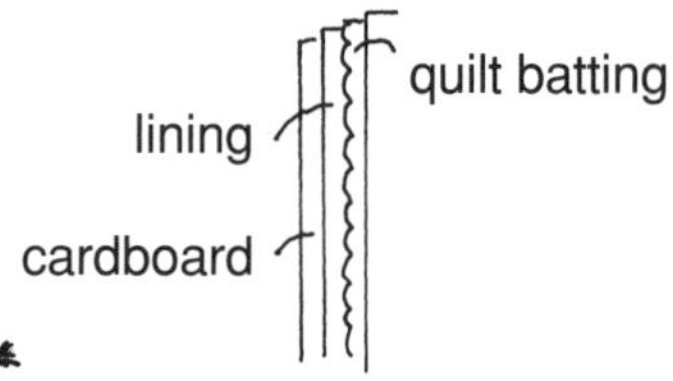

quilt batting
lining
cardboard

Make Silver Grass Leaves

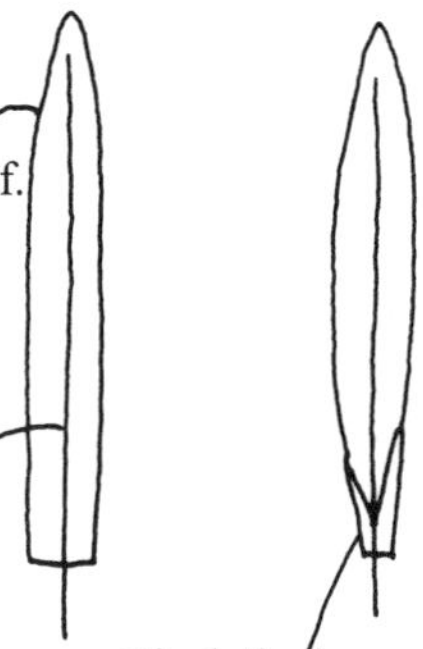

Make in the same manner as flower leaf.
Sandwich #30 stem wire.
Pinch the lower ends of leaf and glue together.

Assemble Flowers and Leaves

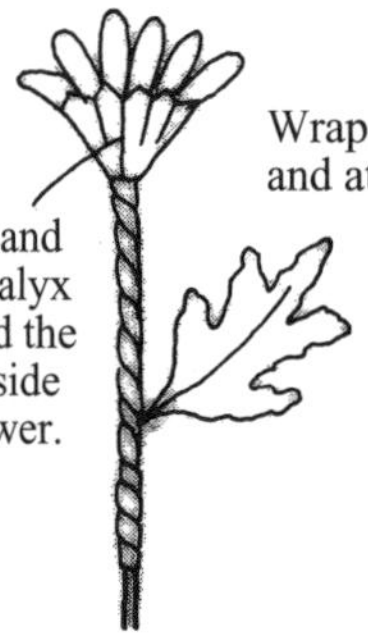

Wrap stem with floral tape and attach leaves.
Wrap and glue calyx around the underside of flower.

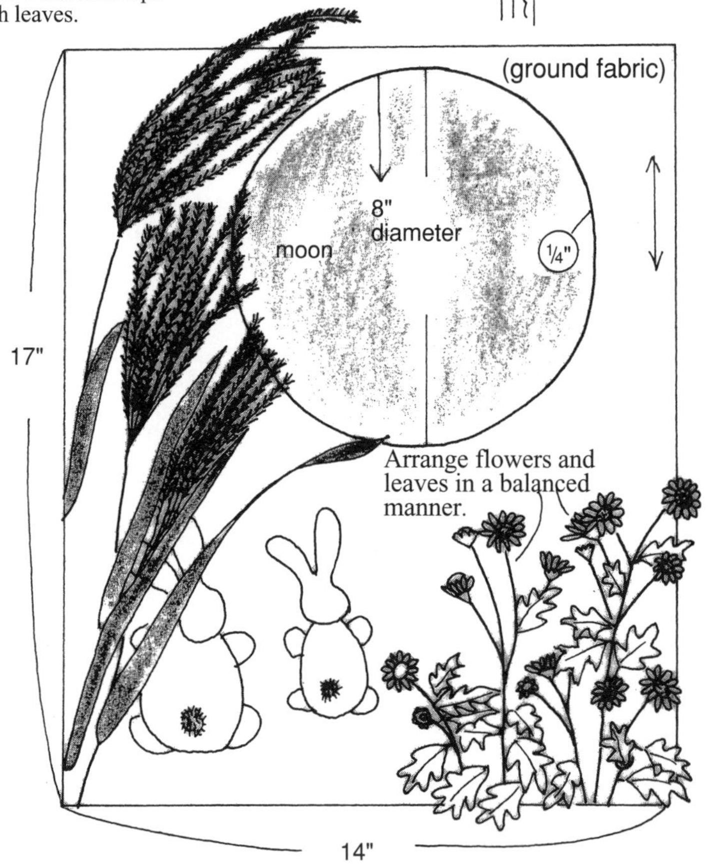

(ground fabric)
8" diameter
moon
1/4"
17"
14"
Arrange flowers and leaves in a balanced manner.

Assemble Silver Grass

Unravel weft threads.

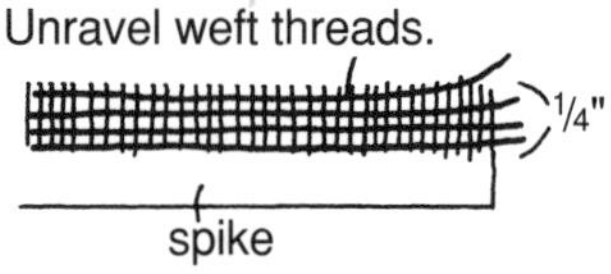

1/4"
spike

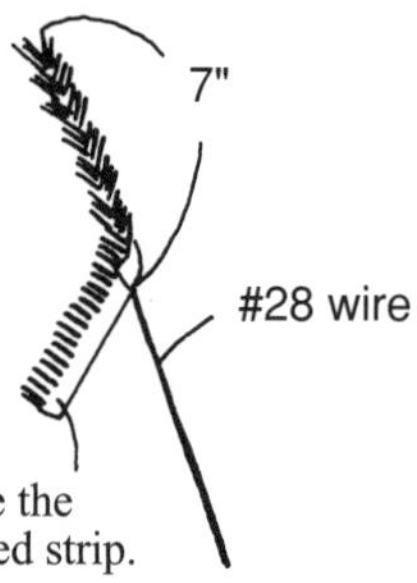

7"
#28 wire
Entwine the unraveled strip.

Assemble 8 to 10 wires and attach to a #20 wire by wrapping with floral tape.

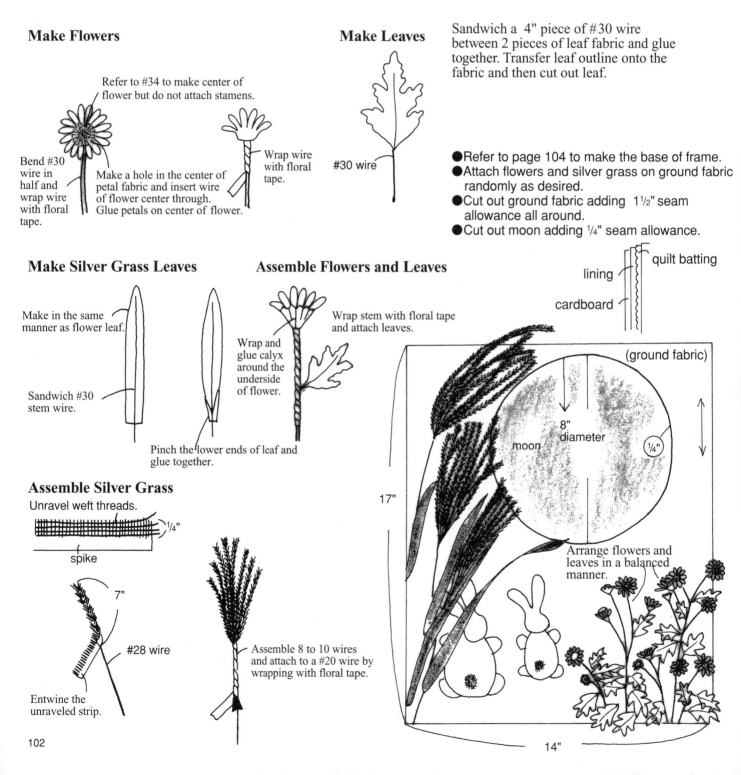

ACTUAL-SIZE PATTERNS AND DRAWINGS
☆Seam allowance included

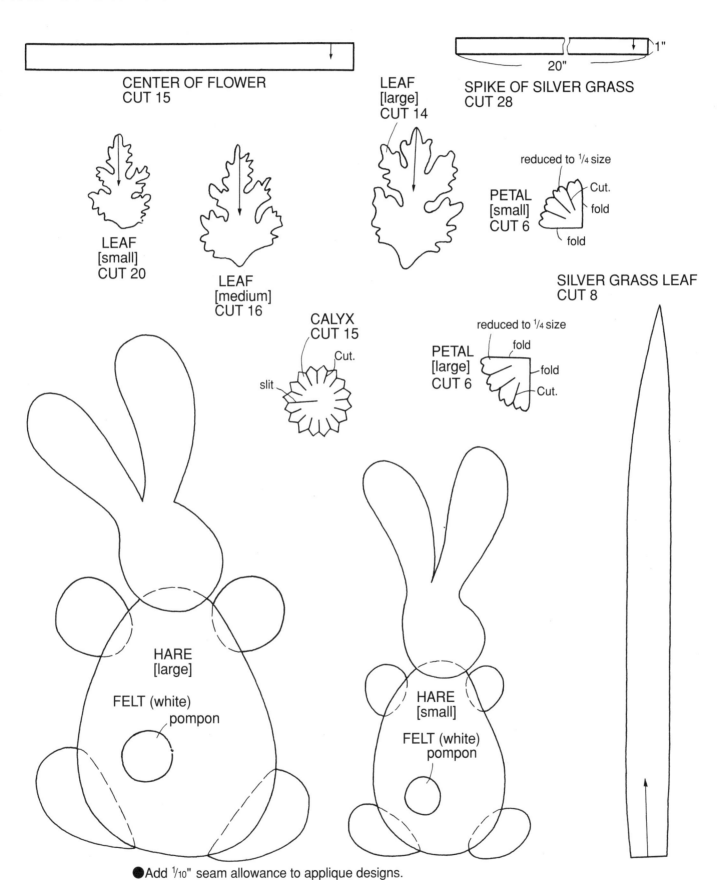

CENTER OF FLOWER
CUT 15

LEAF
[large]
CUT 14

SPIKE OF SILVER GRASS
CUT 28

20"

1"

LEAF
[small]
CUT 20

LEAF
[medium]
CUT 16

reduced to 1/4 size

PETAL
[small]
CUT 6

Cut.

fold

fold

SILVER GRASS LEAF
CUT 8

CALYX
CUT 15

Cut.

slit

reduced to 1/4 size

PETAL
[large]
CUT 6

fold

fold

Cut.

HARE
[large]

FELT (white)
pompon

HARE
[small]

FELT (white)
pompon

●Add 1/10" seam allowance to applique designs.

36 RUDBECKIA SWAYING IN THE BREEZE on page 67

Materials

Petals: 4" x 6" orange print, 2" x 4" yellow print, 2" x 4" yellow fabric, Center of flower: 2" x 6" green check fabric, Buds: 2" x 6" green print, Calyxes: 2" x 8" green fabric, Leaves: 2" x 6" green check fabric, Background: 12" x 10" blue check fabric, 8" x 12" white-base print,

10" x 8" beige print, Chair Applique: Scraps of brown solid, brown check, pink check, printed brown, etc. Backing: 12" x 10" cotton, 12" x 10" quilt batting, 10" x 8" cardboard, 15 #26 stem wires, Embroidery floss (brown, yellow, green), Polyfil, Green floral tape, Craft glue, 10" x 8" picture frame (inner measurements)

Make Background

1. Piece all ground fabrics. Place it over quilt batting and backing. Stitch through all three layers.

2. Applique chair and hat referring to opposite page, and quilt around the applique.

3. Refer to the figures (right) to secure cardboard to the backside.

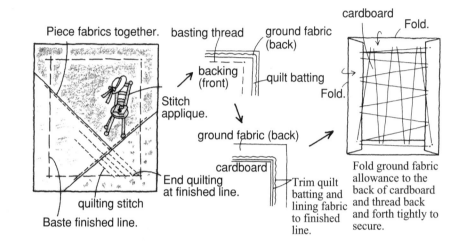

Piece fabrics together.

Baste finished line.

quilting stitch

End quilting at finished line.

Stitch applique.

basting thread

backing (front)

ground fabric (back)

quilt batting

ground fabric (back)

cardboard

Trim quilt batting and lining fabric to finished line.

cardboard

Fold.

Fold.

Fold.

Fold ground fabric allowance to the back of cardboard and thread back and forth tightly to secure.

Make Flowers

1. Make Petals.

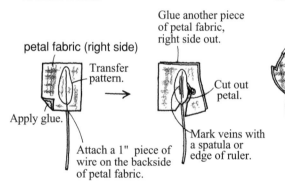

petal fabric (right side)

Transfer pattern.

Apply glue.

Attach a 1" piece of wire on the backside of petal fabric.

Glue another piece of petal fabric, right side out.

Cut out petal.

Mark veins with a spatula or edge of ruler.

2. Make Leaves.

Follow the same procedure to make petals.

Attach a 2"-long #26 stem wire.

3. Make Center of Flower.

Stitch inside edges, leaving 1/8" seam allowance.

Place polyfil in the center

#26 wire

Pull thread to gather.

Make two 14"-long centers of flower and two 7"-long buds.

Attach petals around center of flower with glue.

Cut wire when glue is dry.

4. Attach Calyxes.

Make a hole in the middle of the calyx fabric, insert flower stem through the hole, and glue calyx to the base of flower.

Pull the tips of calyx to show between the petals.

Attach calyx to center of flower with glue.

For buds, make a hole in the middle of calyx fabric, insert flower stem through the hole.

5. Make 4 Different Kinds of Stems.
Attach leaves and buds to stem with floral tape:

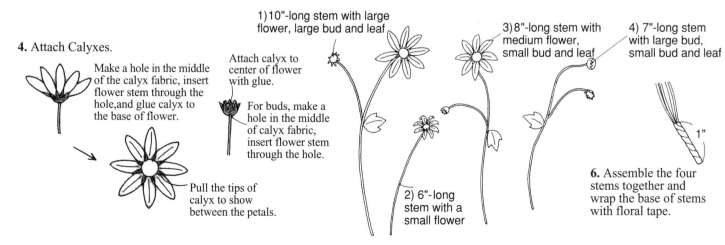

1) 10"-long stem with large flower, large bud and leaf

2) 6"-long stem with a small flower

3) 8"-long stem with medium flower, small bud and leaf

4) 7"-long stem with large bud, small bud and leaf

1"

6. Assemble the four stems together and wrap the base of stems with floral tape.

Preparation of Background Fabric

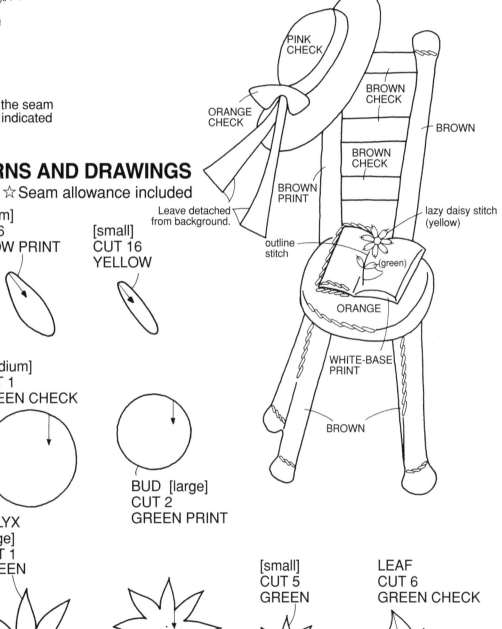

●The numbers encircled represent the seam allowance. Cut out fabric adding the indicated seam allowances.

Actual-size Design for Applique

●Add ⅛" seam allowance.
●Stiffen hat ribbon with glue solution. Do not add seam allowance.
●Use 2-ply embroidery floss. Embroider with outline stitches (brown) unless directed otherwise.

ACTUAL-SIZE PATTERNS AND DRAWINGS

☆Seam allowance included

PETAL
[large]
CUT 16
ORANGE PRINT

[medium]
CUT 16
YELLOW PRINT

[small]
CUT 16
YELLOW

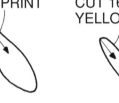

CENTER OF FLOWER
[large] CUT 1
GREEN CHECK

[medium]
CUT 1
GREEN CHECK

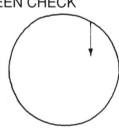

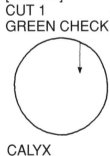

BUD [large]
CUT 2
GREEN PRINT

CALYX
[large]
CUT 1
GREEN

BUD
[small]
CUT 2
GREEN PRINT

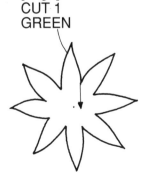

[medium]
CUT 1
GREEN

[small]
CUT 5
GREEN

LEAF
CUT 6
GREEN CHECK

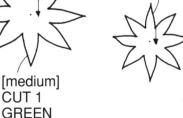

105

37 SONG OF PASSIFLORA on page 67

Materials

Leaves/Calyxes: 6" x 6" green print (A), 4" x 4" green print (B), 2" x 6" green check (C), Petals: 6" x 6" light green polka dot, 2" x 2" red check, Applique: 4" x 4" red check, 2" x 6" blue/red check, 2" x 2" blue print, 1" x 1" red print, Background: 12" x 12" neutral print,

Backing: 12" x 12" cotton, 12" x 12" quilt batting, 7 1/2"x 7 1/2" cardboard, 2 3mm beads, 15 #26 stem wires, Embroidery floss (blue, brown), Polyfil, Green floral tape, Purple felt-tip pen, Craft glue, Awl, 7 1/2" x 7 1/2" picture frame (inner measurements)

Make Passiflora

1. Make Leaves.

2. Make Center of Flower.

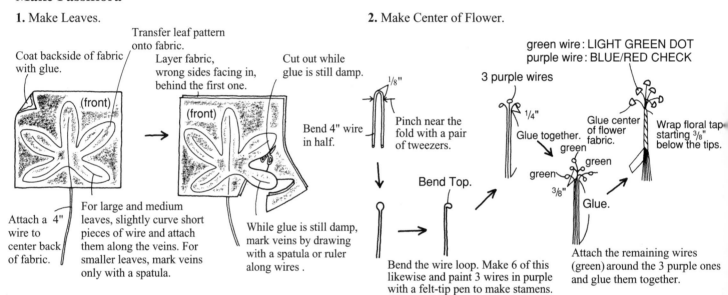

Transfer leaf pattern onto fabric.

Coat backside of fabric with glue.

Layer fabric, wrong sides facing in, behind the first one.

Cut out while glue is still damp.

(front)

(front)

Bend 4" wire in half.

Attach a 4" wire to center back of fabric.

For large and medium leaves, slightly curve short pieces of wire and attach them along the veins. For smaller leaves, mark veins only with a spatula.

While glue is still damp, mark veins by drawing with a spatula or ruler along wires.

1/8"

Pinch near the fold with a pair of tweezers.

Bend Top.

Bend the wire loop. Make 6 of this likewise and paint 3 wires in purple with a felt-tip pen to make stamens.

green wire: LIGHT GREEN DOT
purple wire: BLUE/RED CHECK

3 purple wires

1/4"

Glue together.

green

green

green

3/8"

Glue center of flower fabric.

Wrap floral tape starting 3/8" below the tips.

Glue.

Attach the remaining wires (green) around the 3 purple ones and glue them together.

3. Make Flower.

Stiffen petals with thinned glue. Make petals A and B in the same manner as for leaves. Make a hole in the middle of petal and insert center of flower wire through it, Attach petals with glue.

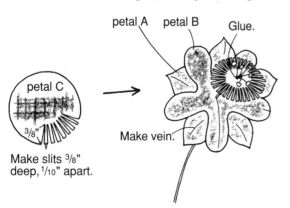

petal A   petal B   Glue.

petal C

3/8"

Make slits 3/8" deep, 1/10" apart.

Make vein.

4. Make Bud.

Stiffen the remaining petal A with thinned glue.

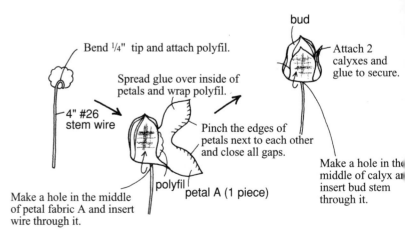

Bend 1/4" tip and attach polyfil.

Spread glue over inside of petals and wrap polyfil.

4" #26 stem wire

Pinch the edges of petals next to each other and close all gaps.

Make a hole in the middle of petal fabric A and insert wire through it.

polyfil

petal A (1 piece)

bud

Attach 2 calyxes and glue to secure.

Make a hole in the middle of calyx and insert bud stem through it.

Applique

1. Make notches at intervals around bird fabric and stitch bird's body and tail on the ground fabric.

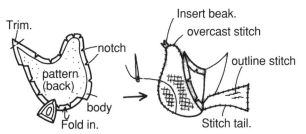

2. Stuff wing with polyfil, and attach to body.

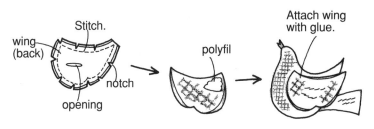

Make Tendrils

To make large tendril, fold a #26 wire in half, wrap with floral tape, and wind wire around an awl.
To make small tendril, wind #26 stem wire around an awl.

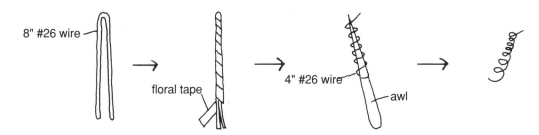

Make Stem

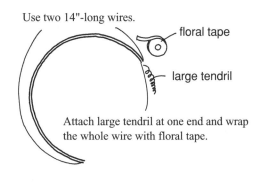

Attach large tendril at one end and wrap the whole wire with floral tape.

Design of Ground Fabric and Quilting Position

- Cut out ground fabric adding a 2½" seam allowance all around.
- Cut out quilt batting and backing fabric as indicated.
- Refer to page 104 for instructions of background.

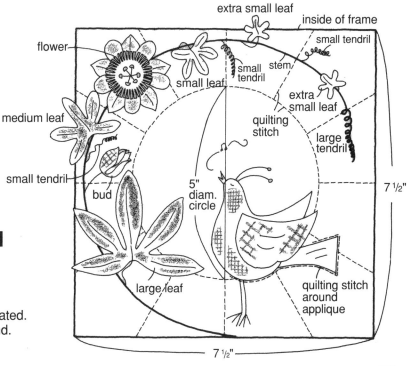

ACTUAL-SIZE PATTERNS AND DRAWINGS

☆Seam allowance included

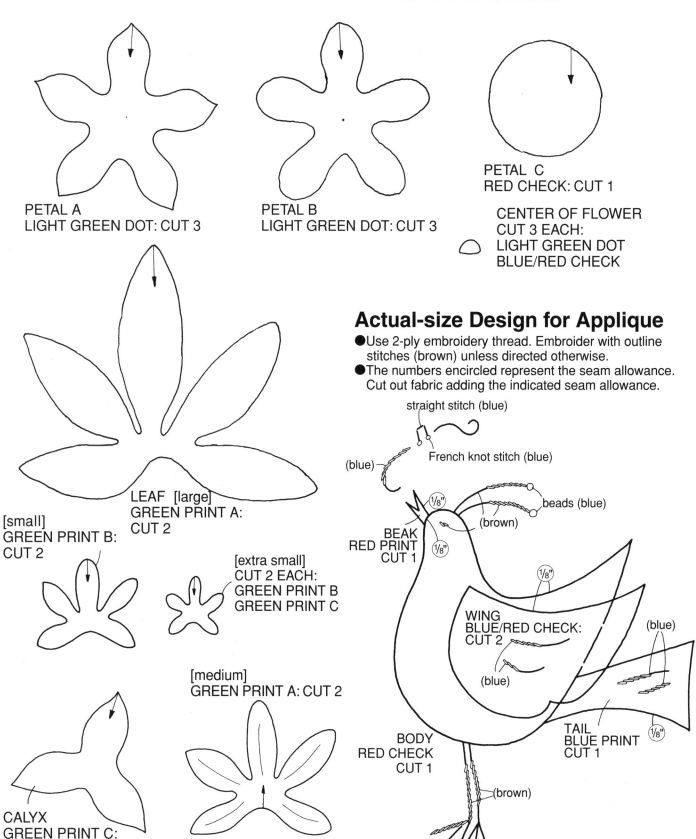

PETAL A
LIGHT GREEN DOT: CUT 3

PETAL B
LIGHT GREEN DOT: CUT 3

PETAL C
RED CHECK: CUT 1

CENTER OF FLOWER
CUT 3 EACH:
LIGHT GREEN DOT
BLUE/RED CHECK

LEAF [large]
GREEN PRINT A:
CUT 2

[small]
GREEN PRINT B:
CUT 2

[extra small]
CUT 2 EACH:
GREEN PRINT B
GREEN PRINT C

[medium]
GREEN PRINT A: CUT 2

CALYX
GREEN PRINT C:
CUT 2

Actual-size Design for Applique

● Use 2-ply embroidery thread. Embroider with outline stitches (brown) unless directed otherwise.
● The numbers encircled represent the seam allowance. Cut out fabric adding the indicated seam allowance.

straight stitch (blue)

French knot stitch (blue)

(blue)

beads (blue)

(brown)

⅛"

BEAK
RED PRINT
CUT 1

⅛"

WING
BLUE/RED CHECK:
CUT 2

⅛"

(blue)

(blue)

BODY
RED CHECK
CUT 1

TAIL
BLUE PRINT
CUT 1

⅛"

(brown)

Materials

Petals: 6" x 8" pink fabric, 10" x 10" pale pink fabric, 6" x 8" polka dot fabric, Leaves: 14" x 4" green fabric, Covering: 22" x 10" floral print, 8" x 8" quilt batting, 20" 10"-wide cotton lace ,

2 14"-long #26 stem wires, Craft glue, 14" x 8" cardboard, Embroidery floss, 1 2"-deep round box with 6" diam. of lid

Cover Box

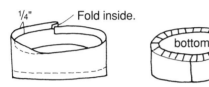

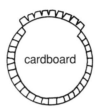

1. Cover the side of box with printed fabric. Allow 1/4" and make notches all around the bottom edges. Fold in top edges. Glue carefully not to make crinkles on the fabric.

2. Cut out two circles from cardboard the same size as the lid of box. Cover each with printed fabric by cutting notches and gluing 1/4" allowance to the box. For the lid, place quilt batting inside to form a mound. Attach flat circle to the bottom of box, and the mounded circle to the lid.

Make Leaves

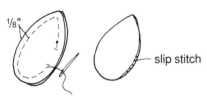

Make Lace Decoration

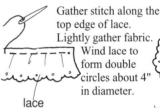

Gather stitch along the top edge of lace. Lightly gather fabric. Wind lace to form double circles about 4" in diameter.

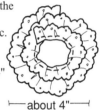

about 4"

1. Layer 2 pieces of leaf fabric, right sides facing, and stitch around fabric leaving 1/8" seam allowance. Leave opening unstitched. Turn right side out and slipstich to close opening.

2. Stitch veins of leaf with 2-ply embroidery floss. Attach a 2"-long wire to the back of the leaf and glue to secure.

ACTUAL-SIZE PATTERNS AND DRAWINGS
☆ Seam allowance included

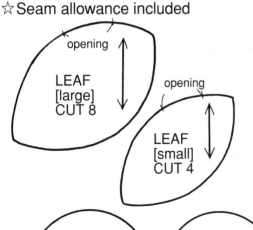

opening

LEAF
[large]
CUT 8

opening

LEAF
[small]
CUT 4

LID
FLORAL PRINT:
CUT 1
6 3/4"

BOTTOM
FLORAL PRINT:
CUT 1
6 1/2"

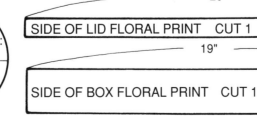

Attach leaves with glue.

Gather-stitch along selvage. Pull thread and knot off. Form double layers of circles with lace strips, and stitch onto the center of lid.

●Rose pattern on page 110, instructions on page 111. Glue on leaves.

20"

SIDE OF LID FLORAL PRINT   CUT 1 — 1"

19"

SIDE OF BOX FLORAL PRINT   CUT 1 — 2 1/2"

40 ROSE BALOON WITH BASKET on page 68

Materials

Petals: 32" x 1.2 yd pink fabric, 32" x 1.2 yd pale pink fabric, 32" x 1.2 yd pink polka dot fabric, Teddy bear: 16" x 6" printed fabric, 5 14"-long #26 stem wires, Craft glue, 1 4"-diam. styrofoam sphere, 12 4mm white pearl beads, 2mm black beads for eyes, 8 commercial floral appliques, 1 miniature ribbon bow, Polyfil, 1 1½"-diam. rattan basket, 6" rattan vine, 16" nylon string, Embroidery floss, 4 ⅜"-diam. buttons

ACTUAL-SIZE PATTERNS AND DRAWINGS

☆ Seam allowance included

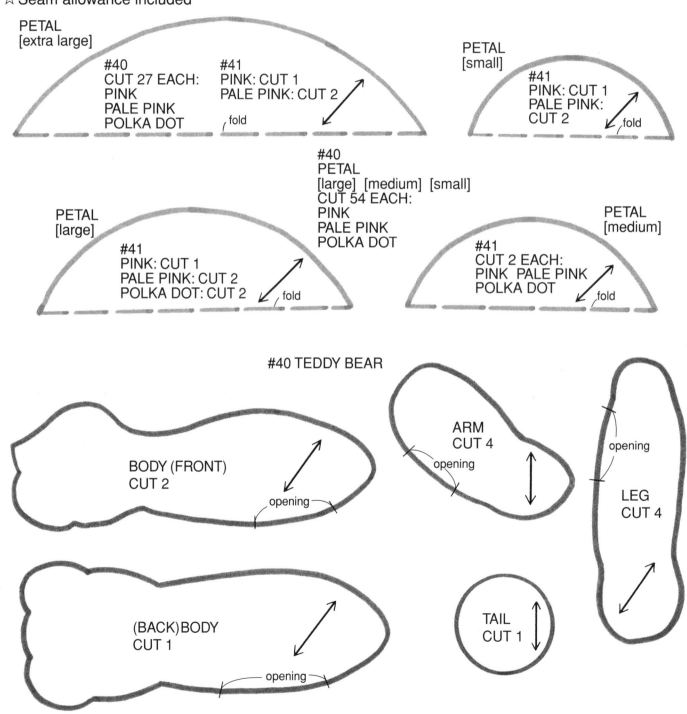

PETAL [extra large]

#40
CUT 27 EACH:
PINK
PALE PINK
POLKA DOT

#41
PINK: CUT 1
PALE PINK: CUT 2

fold

PETAL [small]

#41
PINK: CUT 1
PALE PINK:
CUT 2

fold

#40
PETAL
[large] [medium] [small]
CUT 54 EACH:
PINK
PALE PINK
POLKA DOT

PETAL [large]

#41
PINK: CUT 1
PALE PINK: CUT 2
POLKA DOT: CUT 2

fold

PETAL [medium]

#41
CUT 2 EACH:
PINK PALE PINK
POLKA DOT

fold

#40 TEDDY BEAR

BODY (FRONT)
CUT 2

opening

ARM
CUT 4

opening

opening

LEG
CUT 4

(BACK) BODY
CUT 1

opening

TAIL
CUT 1

Make Roses

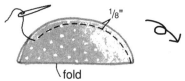 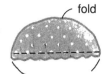

1. Fold petal fabric in half, wrong sides facing in, and gather-stitch along edges, leaving 1/8" seam allowance. Gather fabric to make petals.

Make in 4 sizes:
Extra-large (2")
Large   (1½")
Medium   (1⅛")
Small   (¾")

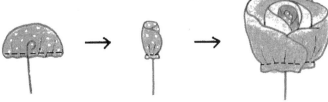

2. Cut the wire into 2¼" and bend ¼" top end. Insert wire into petal fabric and wrap fabric around wire. Glue to secure. Attach successively 2 small, 2 medium, 2 large, and 1 extra-large petals. Secure with glue. Combine colors as desired. Make 81 roses.

Make Teddy Bear

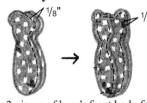 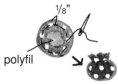

1. Place 2 pieces of bear's front body fabric right sides in. Stitch the center front line. Layer front body and back body right sides facing in, and stitch around edges. Leave opening unstitched and turn fabric right side out. Stuff up with polyfil, and slipstich to close opening.

2. Stitch likewise arms and legs. Stuff up with polyfil and slipstitch to close opening.

polyfil

3. Gather-stitch around tail fabric, leaving 1/8" seam allowance. Place some polyfil in the hollow and pull thread to gather fabric. Knot off.

2mm beads
satin stitch
straight stitch

4. Attach arms and legs to body. Stitch buttons with body parts. Stitch features onto face.

Assembly

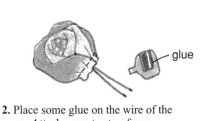

1"
center of bottom

1. Glue 1"-radius pink fabric at the bottom of styrofoam sphere.

glue

2. Place some glue on the wire of the roses. Attach roses to styrofoam sphere. Leave a space of 1"-radius circle at the bottom of sphere. Fill the rest with roses.

3. Tie strings on four equidistant points on the edge of the basket. Glue a pearl on the knots of the string. Attach with glue the ends of the string to 4 points in the lower middle part of the sphere.

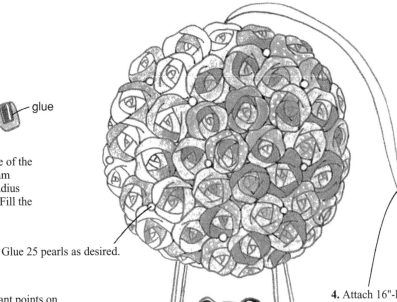

Glue 25 pearls as desired.

Hanging cord: Loop and secure 6"-length of rattan vine with thread.

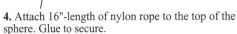

4. Attach 16"-length of nylon rope to the top of the sphere. Glue to secure.

Attach bow to bear with glue.

Attach 8 pearl beads.

Attach commercially-made appliques.

43 GRAPE WREATH on page 69

Materials
Grapes: 20" x 4" purple fabric, 16" x 4" purple floral print, 12" x 4" reddish purple fabric, 16" x 4" pink print, Leaves: 20" x 6" green fabric, 20" x 4" green print,

Batting: 4 yds x 2" quilt batting, 20" x 6" quilt batting, 5 yds 3/8"-wide Bordeaux-color bias tape, 9 14"-long #20 green stem wires, 16 14"-long #26 green stem wires, Craft glue, Polyfil, Dark floral tape

Make Wreath Base

●Refer to page 70 to make base for wreath.

Wrap wire wreath compactly with bias tape at 3/8" interval. Stitch to join both ends of bias tape. Attach the cord for hanging the wreath.

Make Fruit

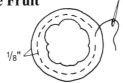

1/8"

1. Stitch around fabric, 1/8" inside of raw edges, and leave thread attached. Place polyfil in the center of the fabric.

Make Leaves

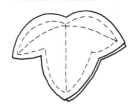

1. Sandwich quilt batting between 2 pieces of leaf fabric, right sides out, and stitch through the three layers.

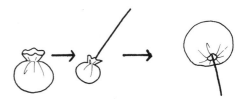

2. Pull thread to gather fabric. Cut #26 stem wire into 2 1/4", place some glue on the edge and insert into polyfil. Tuck in the seam allowance into the fabric ball with the aid of an awl.

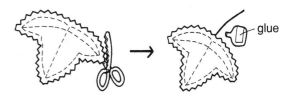

glue

2. Trim leaf edges with pinking shears. Cut #26 stem wire into 2 1/4" and insert into the leaf. Glue the base to secure.

Assembly

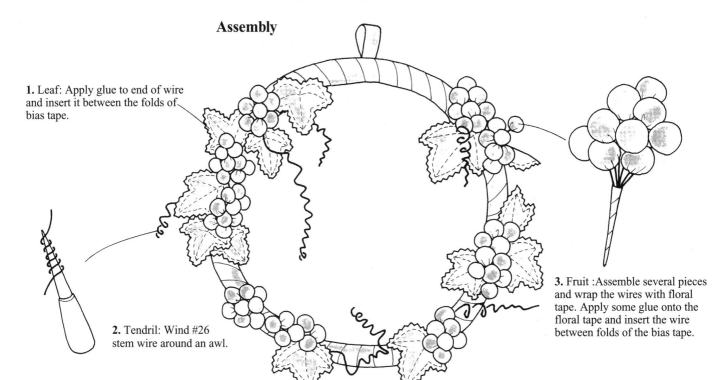

1. Leaf: Apply glue to end of wire and insert it between the folds of bias tape.

2. Tendril: Wind #26 stem wire around an awl.

3. Fruit :Assemble several pieces and wrap the wires with floral tape. Apply some glue onto the floral tape and insert the wire between folds of the bias tape.

ACTUAL-SIZE PATTERNS AND DRAWINGS
☆ Seam allowance included

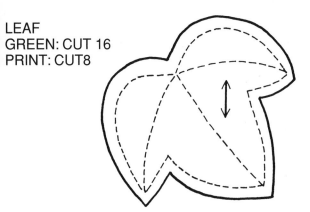

LEAF
GREEN: CUT 16
PRINT: CUT8

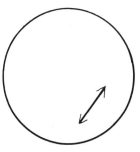

GRAPE
PURPLE: CUT 24
FLORAL PRINT: CUT 20
REDDISH PURPLE: CUT 14
PINK PRINT: CUT 11

44/45 BOUQUET POMANDER AND GLOVES on page 72

MARGUERITE
PETAL

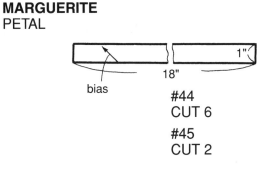

bias
18"
1"

#44
CUT 6

#45
CUT 2

MARGUERITE
CENTER OF FLOWER

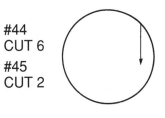

#44
CUT 6

#45
CUT 2

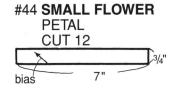

MARGUERITE
CENTER BASE
#44 (CUT 18 BATTING
     CUT 6 CARDBOARD)
#45 (CUT 6 BATTING
     CUT 2 CARDBOARD)

#44 **SMALL FLOWER**
CENTER OF FLOWER
CUT 12

#44 **SMALL FLOWER**
PETAL
CUT 12

bias   7"   ¾"

#44 **SMALL FLOWER**
CENTER BASE
(CUT 36 BATTING
CUT 12 CARDBOARD)

#44 **ROSE**
PETAL
[small]
CUT 39

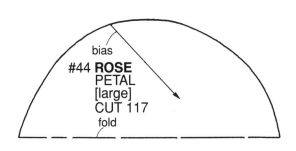

bias
#44 **ROSE**
PETAL
[large]
CUT 117
fold

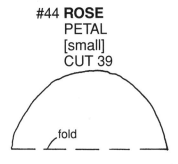

fold

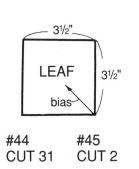

3½"

LEAF   3½"

bias

#44   #45
CUT 31   CUT 2

38/39 ROSE TOPIARY on page 68

●All fabrics are cotton. General supplies such as craft glue, styrofoam sphere (4"-diam.), modeling clay, and packing are common for both #38 and 39.

Materials for #38
Fabric A: 20" x 34" brown fabric
Fabric B: 20" x 34" yellow fabric
Fabric C: 20" x 34" beige fabric
Fabric D: 26" x 20" orange fabric
Fabric E: 8" x 34" green fabric
10 14"-long #24 stem wires, 1 4¾"-diam. unglazed pot,
12"-length twig, Approx. 20" paper cord

Materials for #39
Fabric A: 26" x 34" white fabric
Fabric B: 26" x 34" rose pink fabric
Fabric C: 26" x 34" pale pink fabric
Fabric D: 22" x 34" pink fabric
Fabric E: 16" x 8" red fabric
Fabric F: 22" x 1 yd green fabric
15 14"-long #24 stem wires, 1 4"-diam. unglazed pot,
8"-length twig, Approx. 16" paper cord

Make Roses

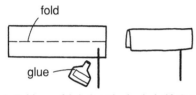    

1. Fold rose fabric lengthwise in half. Cut stem wire into 1½" and insert into the fold of fabric. Glue to secure wire.

2. Wind fabric around wire, easing in order not to make it too tight. Wind thread around the base to secure.

3. Make a slit in the middle of calyx fabric. Attach calyx to the base of the flower with glue.

Assembly

Place some glue on the edge of flower wire and insert it into the styrofoam sphere.
Cover the sphere with flowers filling in any gaps.

ACTUAL-SIZE PATTERNS AND DRAWINGS
☆Seam allowance included

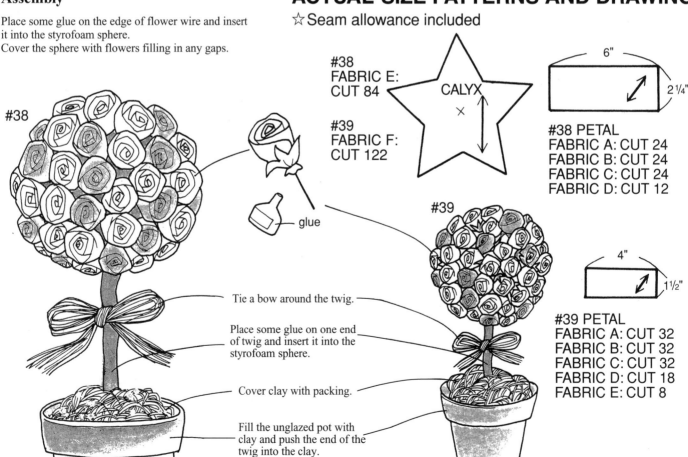

#38
FABRIC E:
CUT 84

#39
FABRIC F:
CUT 122

CALYX
×

6"
2¼"

#38 PETAL
FABRIC A: CUT 24
FABRIC B: CUT 24
FABRIC C: CUT 24
FABRIC D: CUT 12

4"
1½"

#39 PETAL
FABRIC A: CUT 32
FABRIC B: CUT 32
FABRIC C: CUT 32
FABRIC D: CUT 18
FABRIC E: CUT 8

#38

#39

glue

Tie a bow around the twig.

Place some glue on one end of twig and insert it into the styrofoam sphere.

Cover clay with packing.

Fill the unglazed pot with clay and push the end of the twig into the clay.